10/2/09 Scholastic $38.00

yurok

Ecuador

Ecuador

BY JOANN MILIVOJEVIC

Enchantment of the World™
Second Series

Children's Press®

An Imprint of Scholastic Inc.

NEW YORK TORONTO LONDON AUCKLAND SYDNEY
MEXICO CITY NEW DELHI HONG KONG
DANBURY, CONNECTICUT

Frontispiece: A woman in Carabuela knits a pancho.

Consultant: Richard Abisla, International Observer, Civic Council of Grassroots and Indigenous Groups of Honduras

Please note: All statistics are as up-to-date as possible at the time of publication.

Book production by Herman Adler

Library of Congress Cataloging-in-Publication Data

Milivojevic, JoAnn.
   Ecuador / by JoAnn Milivojevic.
      p. cm. — (Enchantment of the world. Second series)
   Includes bibliographical references and index.
   ISBN-13: 978-0-531-20651-5
   ISBN-10: 0-531-20651-3
   1. Ecuador—Juvenile literature. I. Title. II. Series.
   F3708.5.M55 2009
   986.6—dc22   2008044176

SCHOLASTIC, CHILDREN'S PRESS, and associated logos are trademarks and/or registered trademarks of Scholastic Inc.
1 2 3 4 5 6 7 8 9 10 R 19 18 17 16 15 14 13 12 11 10   62

Ecuador

Contents

Cover photo:
Playing a panpipe

Galápagos Islands

La Tolita sculpture

Tradition and Change

8

In the Republic of Ecuador, hats serve many purposes. They help people stay warm, shield people from the sun, and make money for the skilled artisans who create them. But hats also play another important role in Ecuadoran society: they can reveal the cultural group and home region of the people wearing them.

The Otavaleños, who make their home in the area near Quito, wear dark-colored, small-brimmed fedoras made from felt. In the southern Andes Mountains region of Cañar, men wear wide-brimmed, white felt hats. Along the coast, people often

Opposite: **Both fedora hats and baseball caps are popular in Ecuador.**

A woman weaves a Panama hat out of straw.

wear Panama hats, which are made from tightly woven straw. Some of these hat styles date back hundreds of years.

A more contemporary hat has also made its way onto the scene. It's the baseball cap, and it's worn by people throughout Ecuador. It does not reveal a person's cultural heritage, but the baseball cap is a good example of how the cultures of other countries have influenced life in Ecuador.

Locating Ecuador

Ecuador is in northwestern South America. Its neighbor to the north is Colombia, and Peru lies to the east and south. The Pacific Ocean borders Ecuador on the west. With an area of 106,889 square miles (276,840 square kilometers), Ecuador is a little larger than the state of Colorado.

The rocky Galápagos Islands lie 600 miles (1,000 km) west of mainland Ecuador.

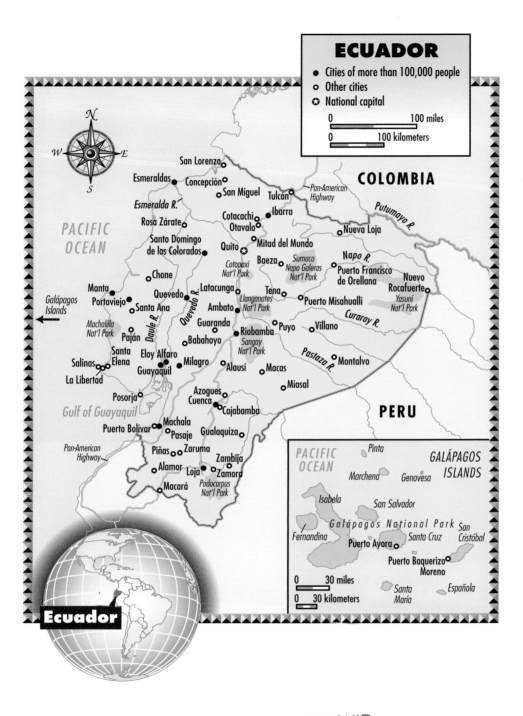

- • Cities of more than 100,000 people
- ○ Other cities
- ⊗ National capital

0   100 miles

0   100 kilometers

COLOMBIA

San Lorenzo
Esmeraldas
Concepción
San Miguel
Tulcán
Pan-American Highway
Esmeralda R.
Cotacachi
Ibarra
Rosa Zárate
Otavalo
Nueva Loja
Putumayo R.
Santo Domingo de los Colorados
Quito
Mitad del Mundo
Napo R.
Baeza
Sumaco Napo Galeras Nat'l Park
PACIFIC OCEAN
Cotopaxi Nat'l Park
Chone
Puerto Francisco de Orellana
Nuevo Rocafuerte
Latacunga
Tena
Yasuní Nat'l Park
Manta
Quevedo
Quevedo R.
Puerto Misahualli
Portoviejo
Ambato
Llanganates Nat'l Park
Santa Ana
Galápagos Islands
Daule R.
Guaranda
Puyo
Curaray R.
Machalilla Nat'l Park
Paján
Babahoyo
Riobamba
Villano
Sangay Nat'l Park
Santa Elena
Eloy Alfaro
Milagro
Pastaza R.
Montalvo
Salinas
Guayaquil
Alausí
Macas
La Libertad
Miasal
Posorja
Azogues
Cuenca
Cajabamba
Gulf of Guayaquil
PERU
Puerto Bolívar
Machala
Gualaquiza
Pasaje
Pan-American Highway
Piñas
Zaruma
Zambija
Alamor
Loja
Zamora
Macará
Podocarpus Nat'l Park

GALÁPAGOS ISLANDS

PACIFIC OCEAN
Pinta
Marchena
Genovesa
Isabela
San Salvador
Galápagos National Park
Fernandina
Puerto Ayora
Santa Cruz
San Cristóbal
Puerto Baquerizo Moreno
Santa María
Española

0   30 miles

0   30 kilometers

Ecuador

San Rafael Falls is the highest waterfall in Ecuador. It plunges about 475 feet (145 m) in the lush forests east of Quito.

Ecuador's landscape is quite diverse. The coasts are lined with sandy beaches and swampy mangrove forests. In the mountains are snowy peaks, misty woods, and magnificent waterfalls. The Amazon rain forest is alive with animals ranging from howler monkeys to anteaters to butterflies.

Strength and Flexibility

Palm trees, which grow in many parts of Ecuador, are both flexible and strong. Palms withstand extreme hurricane winds by bending from side to side without breaking. Like the palm trees, Ecuador must also be flexible and strong. Ecuadorans draw strength from their traditions, their close-knit families, and their deeply held faith. They appreciate their traditional music and crafts.

But Ecuadorans have also learned to be flexible, to change as the world changes. The modern world has brought Ecuador new jobs and new conveniences, such as cell phones and the Internet. As Ecuador moves forward, its people must continue to balance the best of the old with the best of the new.

Some Ecuadorans live traditional lives in rural areas. Others live in large cities and shop at massive malls like this one in Guayaquil.

A Varied Land

ECUADOR CAN BE DIVIDED INTO FOUR DISTINCT GEO-graphic regions. Three of the regions are on the South American mainland, and the fourth is an island chain off the coast.

The Costa region is a narrow stretch of land along the Pacific Ocean. Costa is Spanish for "coast." Inland from there is the Sierra, which means "mountain range." In this region, the Andes Mountains extend like a bumpy spine down the center of the country. In the east is the Oriente, the "east." Much of this fairly flat region is covered by Amazonian rain forest. Ecuador's fourth region is a string of islands about 600 miles (1,000 km) to the west of the mainland called the Galápagos Islands.

Opposite: **Ecuador's highest peaks are in the northern part of the country.**

The Galápagos Islands feature beautiful beaches and dramatic rock formations.

The Middle of the World

The equator is an imaginary line that runs around the middle of the globe, lying at an equal distance from the North and South poles. Ecuador takes its name from this imaginary line. The Spanish word *ecuador* means "equator."

The equator runs through the Intiñan Solar Museum in Pichincha, just north of Quito, Ecuador's capital. Museum visitors can straddle a thick red line that marks the equator, putting one foot in the Northern Hemisphere and the other foot in the Southern Hemisphere.

The Costa

The coastal lowlands account for about one-quarter of Ecuador's land area. The Costa extends from the Colombian border in the north to the southern port city of Guayaquil and spreads east to the Andes Mountains. Its width varies from 7 to 124 miles (11 to 200 km).

Guayaquil is the largest city and largest port in Ecuador.

The average annual temperature in the Costa is 77 degrees Fahrenheit (25° Celsius). The northern part of the Costa is more humid, and the south is drier. Each year, up to 80 inches (200 centimeters) of rain falls on the northern Costa area.

Ecuador's Geographical Features

Area: 106,889 square miles (276,840 sq km)

Lowest Elevation: Sea level, along the Pacific Ocean

Highest Elevation: Mount Chimborazo, 20,565 feet (6,268 m) above sea level

Longest Navigable River: Napo River, 700 miles (1,100 km) through Ecuador and Peru

Highest Waterfall: San Rafael Falls, 475 feet (145 m)

Highest Volcano: Cotopaxi, 19,347 feet (5,897 m)

Wettest Area: The Oriente, with up to 100 inches (250 cm) of precipitation per year

Average High Temperatures: In Quito, 66°F (19°C) in January and 67°F (19°C) in July; in Guayaquil, 88°F (31°C) in January and 84°F (29°C) in July

Average Low Temperatures: In Quito, 50°F (10°C) in January and 49°F (9°C) in July; in Guayaquil, 70°F (21°C) in January and 66°F (19°C) in July

Ecuador's rain forests are filled with dense and varied plant life.

In this northern area, thick tropical rain forests cover the land, and mangroves, trees that can grow in salt water, line much of the shore. Farther south are long, sandy beaches. Forests and grasslands cover the southern coast, which receives an average of about 40 inches (100 cm) of rain a year.

On Shaky Ground

Regions that lie on the borders of the tectonic plates that make up Earth's outer layer are prone to earthquakes. The Pacific Ocean is ringed with the borders of tectonic plates. Ninety percent of the world's earthquakes and 80 percent of its largest earthquakes occur around this ring.

Ecuador has suffered some devastating earthquakes during its history. In 1797, a quake hit the town of Cajabamba, completely destroying it. An earthquake in 1923 damaged nearly every house in Tulcán, a market town on the border with Colombia. In 1987, an earthquake struck the Oriente region, rupturing an oil pipeline. The oil seeped into the soil and rivers, harming the environment.

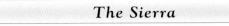

The Sierra

Earth's outer layer is divided into huge pieces called tectonic plates. These plates are constantly moving, and over time, their movement can build mountains. The Andes Mountains rose as two plates collided some 90 million years ago. Earthquakes and volcanic activity frequently occur along the borders between tectonic plates. In Ecuador, this activity is strongest in the Sierra.

The Sierra is the mountainous region in the middle of the country. The Ecuadoran Andes consists of two main ranges that run parallel to each other, extending in a long line

Snow fills the crater of Cotopaxi, a towering volcano about 50 miles (80 km) south of Quito. The volcano last erupted in 1940.

from north to south. The highest peak in Ecuador is Mount Chimborazo, which reaches 20,565 feet (6,268 meters).

About forty volcanoes pepper the Ecuadoran Sierra. Cotopaxi, the highest active volcano in Ecuador, soars to 19,347 feet (5,897 m). The world's most active volcano, fiery Sangay, rises to 17,159 feet (5,230 m) and often spews red-hot lava, ash, and smoke.

Lava flows down Tungurahua volcano in central Ecuador.

As destructive as Ecuador's volcanoes can be, their fine ash helps improve the quality of the soil. The central valley that lies between the two ranges is fertile, and people have been farming it for thousands of years. The average elevation in the central valley is roughly 8,000 feet (2,400 m). The rivers that flow down to it from the snowy Andes Mountains provide plenty of water for people, livestock, and plants.

Many farmers in Ecuador's central valley raise alpacas.

Baños

The town of Baños lies high in the Andes near Tungurahua Volcano. Baños means "baths" in Spanish, and visitors enjoy bathing in this town's bubbling hot springs. The volcano heats the water in the springs, and the minerals in the water are believed to have healing properties. In 1999, the townspeople had to be evacuated because Tungurahua erupted, spitting out hot lava and ash dangerously close to town. But the area still attracts people who love to bathe in the naturally heated waters.

The Oriente

East of the Sierra are the Amazonian rain forests and rivers of the Oriente region. This region accounts for about half the land in Ecuador. The Oriente is filled with thick, hot, damp forests. It is rich with wildlife and plants. More than 500 species of birds live in the Napo region, in the northeast.

Though animals and plants thrive in the hot, humid rain forests, not many people live there. Traditionally, a few isolated indigenous, or native, groups made their homes in the dense forest areas. But recently, oil companies began to change the landscape, and more people have moved into the region to work in the oil industry. In 1987, an earthquake broke the pipeline that carries oil from the Oriente to the coast. Huge amounts of oil spilled, damaging the environment.

Many rivers flow through the Oriente, meandering east to join the mighty Amazon River. The longest, the Napo, runs for approximately 700 miles (1,100 km) through Ecuador and Peru. During the rainy season, the rivers of the Oriente swell and flood the land. When the waters recede, they leave behind nutrients that enrich the soil. The rivers are also a means of transportation. Some indigenous peoples, such as the Waorani, live near rivers and travel in dugout canoes. Tourists also visit the rain forest by boat.

A boat travels along the Napo River in Ecuador's Oriente region. The Napo eventually flows into the Amazon.

The Galápagos Islands

The Galápagos Islands are a group of volcanic islands about 600 miles (1,000 km) west of mainland Ecuador. The Galápagos chain consists of 13 main islands and many smaller islets, some of them no more than large rocks poking out of the ocean.

The largest island, Isabela, is 75 miles (120 km) long. It is home to the highest point on the islands, Wolf Volcano, which rises 5,610 feet (1,710 m). Lava flows from a 2005 eruption are still visible today as twisting black tracks on the volcano's slopes.

Because the Galápagos are so distant from the mainland, many plants and animals that live there are found nowhere else in the world. Scientists call the Galápagos a living laboratory.

The Galápagos Islands consists of 13 main islands, 6 smaller islands and dozens of rocky islets jutting out of the water.

People enjoy a pleasant day in Guayaquil. The city is often hot and humid.

Climate

Because of the wide-ranging environments and altitudes in Ecuador, temperatures vary dramatically. Quito is in the mountains, and its average high temperature in January is just 66°F (19°C). In Guayaquil, along the southern coast, January is much hotter, with temperatures averaging 88°F (31°C). In July, low temperatures average 49°F (9°C) in Quito and 66°F (19°C) in Guayaquil.

In early 2008, heavy rain produced massive flooding that devastated Babahoyo and other cities in the coastal region. The flooding forced more than 300,000 people from their homes.

Most parts of Ecuador have a wet season and a dry season. The wet, or rainy, season runs roughly from December to June, though its length varies depending on location. In Guayaquil, rain falls more than 20 days a month in January through March, and the dry-season months of August and September receive virtually no rain. During the rainy season, low-lying areas sometimes flood, washing out roads and making travel difficult. Floods in 1998 and 1999 destroyed many beaches, trees, and buildings.

Looking at Ecuador's Cities

With a population of almost 2 million, Guayaquil is the largest city in Ecuador. This coastal city is a major port and the financial center of the country. It is also a lively city filled with clubs where people can dance the night away.

Ecuador's second-largest city is Quito, the capital, which sits in the north-central part of the country. Cuenca (below), the third-largest city, is located in the southern Sierra region at an altitude of 8,468 feet (2,581 m). Home to about 600,000 people, it is a lovely city that features many well-preserved Spanish colonial buildings. Cuenca is considered one of the cultural capitals of Ecuador. It is home to four universities and is a center for artists who make ceramics, blankets, and hats.

With a population of about 200,000, the southern coastal city of Machala is the nation's fourth-largest city. The city is known as the "banana capital of the world" because it lies at the heart of Ecuador's banana-producing region and is a main distribution center of bananas. *El Bananero*, a statue of a man carrying a large branch of bananas, stands on the main road into town.

Natural Wonders

I N THE AMAZON RAIN FOREST, MONKEYS PLAY IN THE TREE-tops, and lines of hardworking ants march across the forest floor. A condor floats on air currents high above snowy mountainsides, while far out in the ocean on the Galápagos Islands, a huge tortoise lumbers across the rocks. Ecuador is alive with many different kinds of plants and animals. Scientists believe that more species live in Ecuador than in any other country in the world. Each geographic region has its own unique wildlife.

Opposite: **The ocelot is one of seven large cat species that live in Ecuador.**

Pygmy marmosets live in Ecuador and other South American nations. They are the smallest monkeys in the world, with bodies that measure just 5 inches (13 cm) long.

Life in the Rain Forest

Along the eastern foothills of the Andes Mountains is the Amazon rain forest, which has more diversity of plant and animal life than anywhere else in the world. Plants crowd the rain forest. On the forest floor are brightly colored flowers called heliconias. Some are red and yellow, and others are delicate shades of pink. They are relatives of the banana, which also grows in the rain forest.

Heliconias produce waxy, brightly colored bracts, which are actually a kind of leaf. Small flowers grow inside the bracts.

Plants Galore

Ecuador has a remarkable diversity of plant life. In the Coca River region of eastern Ecuador, there are more than 6,000 known plant species and many more yet to be discovered. A North American forest typically has fewer than 4,500 species.

Because of the dense plant life in rain forests, trees have to grow tall to reach the sunlight that they need. The treetops form a canopy over the rest of the forest. From high above in an airplane, the top of the canopy looks like bunches of broccoli. In the rain forest, some animals live in the thick trees and never touch the ground. Others live on the ground and never see the sky.

The tops of the trees in the Amazon rain forest form a thick canopy.

The jaguar is the third-largest cat in the world. Only lions and tigers are bigger.

Many kinds of monkeys live in the forest. These include tiny pygmy marmosets, the world's smallest monkey, which are only 5 to 8 inches (13 to 20 cm) tall. The much larger spider monkeys hang out in large groups of 100 or more along riverbanks. Spider monkeys sometimes throw sticks and fruit at people paddling by in canoes. Howler monkeys emit loud calls to define their territory. They are the world's loudest land animals—their calls can be heard 3 miles (5 km) away!

Other residents of the rain forest include cats, such as pumas and jaguars; snakes, such as tree boas; the South American tapir, which is the largest land mammal on the continent; the toothless armadillo, which has a shield of armor made of bony plates; and the spectacled bear, South America's only bear, which got its name from the rings around its eyes that look like glasses.

Many rivers flow through the rain forest. Creatures found in the rivers include caimans, which are members of the alligator family, and piranhas, fish with razor-sharp teeth. Contrary to popular belief, piranhas do not attack people. They tend to be scavengers, feeding on the remains of dead animals. On the other hand, people have been known to eat piranhas and save their teeth as souvenirs.

The dwarf caiman is the smallest member of the alligator family. Males grow to about 4.5 feet (1.3 m) long.

In Ecuador, some traditional healers use rain forest plants to help people get well. They know exactly which roots, flowers, and bark can be used to treat different illnesses. Many of the medicines found in North American drugstores originally came from the natural world. Aspirin, for example, was first made from the bark of the white willow tree. Many other cures may yet be discovered among the thousands of plant species in the Amazon.

Yasuní National Park

Ecuador has 22 national parks, which protect about 17 percent of the nation's land. These protected areas help ensure that the plants and animals that live in them are safe and will have a home in the future. Yasuní National Park lies in the lush rain forest of northeastern Ecuador, between the Napo and the Curary rivers. This park boasts extraordinary diversity. More than 900 species of trees have been identified in a small, 5-acre (2-hectare) plot. They include the ceibo, which grows up to 150 feet (45 m) tall, making it the tallest tree in the rain forest. The park is also home to creatures ranging from the rare giant otter to the tiny broadheaded tree frog (right).

The Amazon also hides another precious resource: oil. To reach the oil, which lies underground, large tracts of forest must be cut down. This destruction forces animals to move to new areas. Some parts of the Amazon have been protected from industry. But oil provides jobs and helps the country's economy. This sometimes overrides concerns about the long-term health of the forest. For now, Ecuador is trying to maintain a delicate balance between economic development and environmental protection.

Oil has been discovered beneath the rain forest in Ecuador. Drilling is important to the nation's economy but destructive to the environment.

The National Bird

The graceful Andean condor is Ecuador's national bird. With its 10-foot (3 m) wingspan, it is one of the largest birds in the world. Like other members of the vulture family, it is a scavenger. It eats the remains of sheep, goats, and other animals.

The Mountain Tapir

Tapirs look like huge pigs with snouts, stubby tails, and large toes. Mountain tapirs, the smallest type of tapir, grow up to 6 feet (1.8 m) long and stand about 3 feet (1 m) high. They weigh as much as 500 pounds (225 kilograms). Tapirs live in the cool cloud forests. Their thick, woolly fur helps keep them warm.

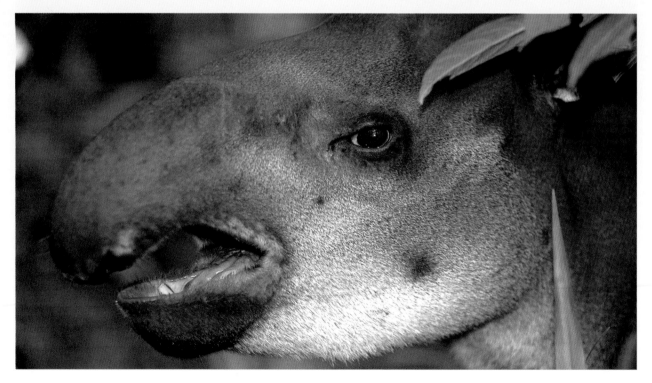

Life in the Mountains

Most of the Andes are forested except for the highest peaks. Lichens growing on rocks are about all that live on the icy peaks. Humid forests with pine trees and grasses grow lower down the mountains, at about 11,000 feet (3,400 m). Ducks, gulls, sparrow hawks, and other birds live in this region, and the Andean condor—Ecuador's national bird—sometimes soars around the mountains. Few land animals live on the mountain's higher elevations, but there are some rodents, foxes, and wild guinea pigs.

Clouds often become trapped in the lower valleys of the mountains, at elevations ranging from about 3,000 to 11,000 feet (900 to 3,400 m). Some forests are permanently cloud-covered. In these cloud forests, the misty air feeds ferns, orchids, and other plants. From toucans to frogs, from tapirs to hummingbirds, a great variety of creatures live in the cloud forests.

Low-hanging clouds provide moisture to the thick vegetation of the rain forest.

Life Along the Shore

Mangrove trees grow in swampy land along the shoreline of the Costa region. Mangrove swamps are breeding grounds for fish. Underwater, the roots of the trees create a protective, wooden web. Baby fish spend their early lives amid the mangrove roots where big fish can't reach them. Mangrove trees also block surging waves during storms, helping protect the shoreline.

About 25 percent of Ecuador's mangrove swamps have been destroyed to create ponds where shrimps are raised. In an effort to protect the mangroves, the government has made it illegal to destroy them. Local villages and international groups have fought against the illegal clearing of mangrove forests. Environmentalists have been teaching farmers how to establish shrimp farms farther from the shoreline, preserving the mangroves.

Tourists explore a mangrove forest in the Galápagos.

Galápagos Life

The Galápagos, a string of volcanic islands off the coast of Ecuador, are home to some unique animals that live and breed only on these rocky outposts. The Galápagos Islands include a wide variety of ecosystems, ranging from arid regions filled with cacti to more humid areas where ferns and orchids grow. The islands support 228 plant species not found anywhere else in the world.

The islands are also home to 28 species of birds found only there, including mangrove finches and Galápagos penguins. Many other birds live part of the year in the Galápagos. These include the blue-footed booby and the yellow-billed waved albatross. The Galápagos lava gull is one of the rarest gulls on earth. Only a few hundred of them remain on the islands.

Darwin in the Galápagos

In 1832, at age 27, English naturalist Charles Darwin visited the remote Galápagos Islands. What he learned there would forever change the way people think about life. Darwin observed the finches and other animals in the Galápagos. He noticed that the finches on each island were slightly different from those on the other islands. On one island where fruit and buds grew, the finches had large, clawlike beaks that could grind down the food. On an island where the finches ate insects that they pulled from holes, the birds had long, narrow beaks.

These observations prompted Darwin to wonder about the nature of similar but distinct species. He concluded that the natural variation among individual finches made some better able to gather food than others. Those that were best suited to gathering food on any given island would have more offspring, thus passing on the helpful trait, such as a long, narrow beak. As these helpful variations were passed down through generations, the species slowly changed. They evolved

to fit their environment. Darwin's theory of evolution became the foundation of modern biology.

Many reptiles live on the Galápagos Islands. Iguanas lie on rocks to catch the warm rays of the sun, as giant Galápagos tortoises munch on grasses and cacti. These land turtles can live more than 100 years.

Ecuador's government declared the Galápagos Islands a national park in 1959. The same year, UNESCO (the United Nations Educational, Scientific, and Cultural Organization) created the Charles Darwin Foundation for the Galápagos.

This foundation created a research station to help support visiting scientists and improve conservation awareness. A big part of the foundation's efforts is focused on preserving the Galápagos tortoise. Scientists have established a breeding program that has had some success in hatching babies.

Each year, more and more people visit the Galápagos Islands. Visitors help boost the local economy. But more visitors means more trash and more damage to the land. Ecuador is working to encourage responsible tourism that protects the very plants and animals that draw visitors to the islands.

A fully grown Galápagos tortoise can weigh 650 pounds (300 kg).

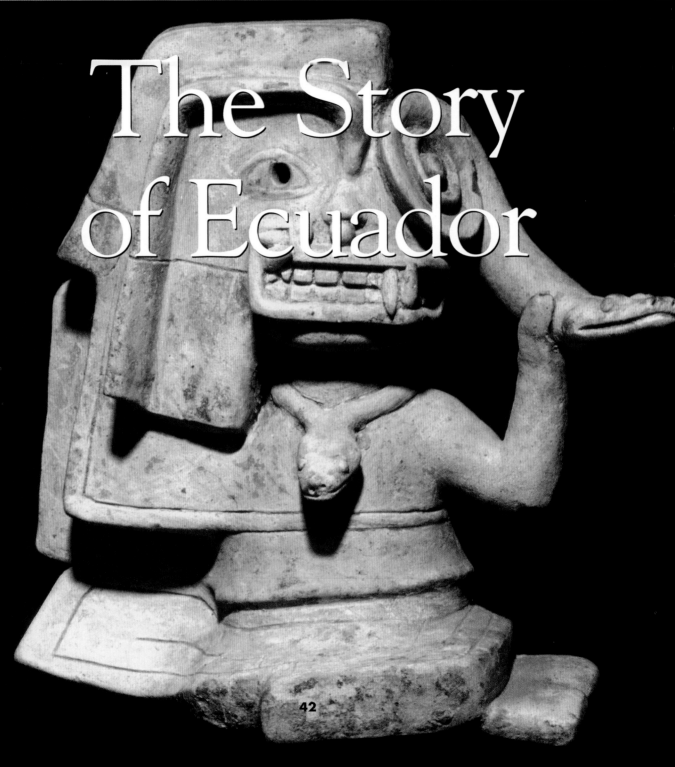

The Story
of Ecuador

42

EXPERTS BELIEVE THAT HUMANS HAVE LIVED IN ECUADOR for more than 10,000 years. The first people in Ecuador were nomads, who wandered the land hunting animals and gathering plants to eat.

Opposite: **This sculpture was produced by the culture of La Tolita.**

Early Peoples

The Las Vegas culture, which dates back to about 9,000 to 6,000 BCE, was one of the first to emerge in what is now Ecuador. The Las Vegas people were fishers, hunters, and gatherers who lived near the Santa Elena Peninsula, on the southern coast. They turned animal bones into tools for fishing and simple farming. Today, 21 Las Vegas sites have been identified on the peninsula.

The Valdivia culture emerged around 3000 BCE. Valdivians are believed to have developed the first pottery in the region. They made figurines of people and carved designs into various colored clays. Scholars think that they may have migrated

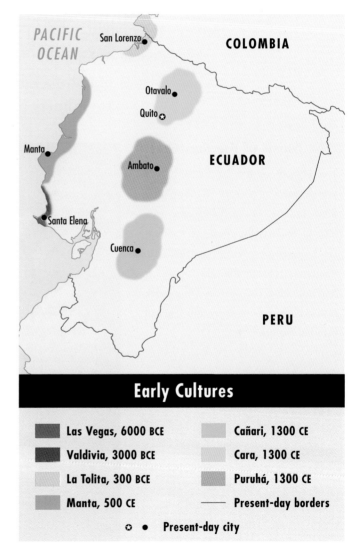

Early Cultures

■ Las Vegas, 6000 BCE		▨ Cañari, 1300 CE
■ Valdivia, 3000 BCE		▨ Cara, 1300 CE
▨ La Tolita, 300 BCE		▨ Puruhá, 1300 CE
■ Manta, 500 CE		— Present-day borders
✪ ● Present-day city		

The Story of Ecuador **43**

from the Amazon to settle along the coast. Valdivians traded with other coastal groups in the area. Their largest settlement was in the Real Alto region, where archaeologists have dug up remains of more than 100 households. They believe that more than 20 people lived in each of the houses.

Around 500 BCE, other coastal cultures began emerging. The culture of La Tolita reached its peak about 300 BCE. The people of La Tolita lived on an island off the coast of the area that is now Esmeraldas Province in northern Ecuador. They were extraordinary artists who created beautiful objects out of

The Mask of the Sun God

The people of the La Tolita culture worshipped the sun. Among the most impressive La Tolita archaeological finds is the mask of the Sun God. Made of gold, it features long, radiating rays of the sun around a fierce-looking face. Today, this mask is used as a symbol by the Central Bank of Ecuador.

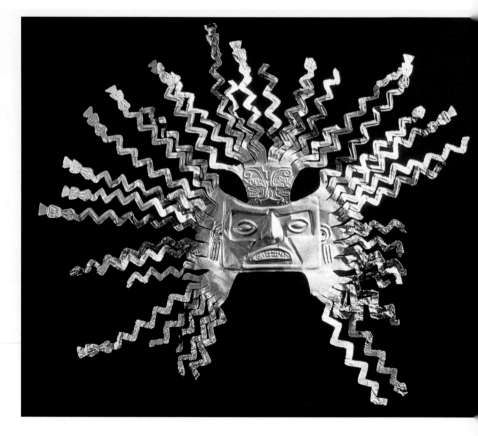

gold, silver, copper, and platinum. Many of their intricately carved gold and silver objects have been found in the province. Archaeologists believe that this area was a burial site and the jewelry and other precious objects were buried with the bodies of deceased people so that they could take them to the next world.

In about 500 CE, the Manta culture emerged along the coast. The Manteños were expert fishers and sailors. They made large rafts from lightweight balsa wood, hung cotton sails on masts, and sailed as far away as Mexico to trade their goods. Because pottery pieces found on the Galápagos Islands look like those made by Manta artists, some archaeologists suspect that the Manteños stopped at the Galápagos.

Emerging around 1300 CE were the Cañari people in the south and the Cara and the Puruhá in the north. Together, they created the Quitu Kingdom.

Inca Invasion and Rule

The Inca arose in what is now southern Peru in the 1200s. Within 300 years, they had conquered many neighboring groups, creating a large, powerful empire. The Inca Empire eventually ruled parts of Bolivia, Chile, Argentina, and Ecuador. The Inca entered Ecuador about 1460. Though the Inca were fierce warriors, it was no simple task to take the land from the Cañaris. The two groups battled for several years. Finally, in 1472, the Inca emperor Tupac Yupanqui and his forces defeated the Cañaris. To reduce competition, he killed most of the male Cañaris and married a Cañari princess.

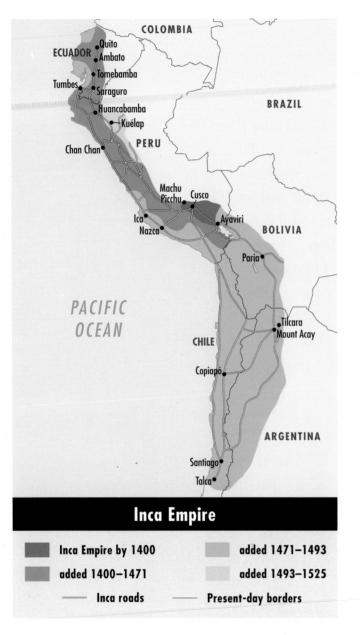

Inca Empire

▇	Inca Empire by 1400	▇	added 1471–1493
▇	added 1400–1471	▇	added 1493–1525
—	Inca roads	—	Present-day borders

The Inca were strategic rulers. If newly conquered people didn't cooperate, the Inca shipped them off to other parts of the empire. That made it difficult for people who had been conquered to organize and challenge the local Inca leaders.

The official language of the Inca was Quechua. It is still spoken today by some people in Ecuador. The Inca introduced more than just their language to the region. They also brought new crops, such as sweet potatoes, coca, and peanuts, and a very helpful animal, the llama. People used llamas to work their fields, and they used llama wool to make yarn that they wove into colorful fabrics.

The Inca built many roads, including the Imperial Highway, which extended 1,230 miles (1,980 km) from Quito to Cusco, Peru, the capital of the Inca Empire. The Inca people had a system of taxation called *mita*. Under the mita system, people didn't pay money. Instead, they paid in goods or services. Helping build a road was one way people could pay their mita.

Remains of the Inca

Ecuador is home to several Inca archaeological sites. In the 1500s, the Inca emperor Tupac Yupanqui began building a huge city called Tomebamba, but the Spanish invasion interrupted its construction. Today, the city of Cuenca sits atop the ruins of Tomebamba.

Ingapirca (below) is in the southern mountains. It is the best-preserved Inca site in all of Ecuador. Ingapirca's highlights include the round Temple of the Sun. The site also features parts of a fortress, a storehouse, and other structures.

Fall of the Inca, Rise of Spain

Tupac Yupanqui and his Cañari wife had a son named Huayna, who inherited his father's throne. After Huayna died, his son Atahualpa fought his half-brother Huascar for control of the empire. Atahualpa eventually triumphed, but the civil war had weakened the empire.

Huayna ruled the Inca Empire in the early 16th century.

Spanish conquistador (conqueror) Francisco Pizarro arrived in Peru in 1532, just as the Inca Empire was vulnerable. Pizarro tricked Atahualpa into meeting him. Instead of the promised friendly discussion, Pizarro captured Atahualpa. The Inca leader offered Pizarro two rooms filled with silver and gold in exchange for his freedom. Pizarro agreed and took the treasure. But instead of setting Atahualpa free, he had him killed, in 1533.

Pizarro told his lieutenant Sebastián de Belalcázar to ship the treasure to a Spanish colony in Panama, the narrowest part of Central America. News of the loot reached Pedro de Alvarado, a Spanish explorer in search of gold. He set out from Guatemala, north of Panama, with the plan of stealing the riches, and then conquering Quito. Alvarado and 500 men arrived at Manta, on the central Ecuadoran coast, in 1534. They killed any indigenous people who crossed their path. Historians estimate that hundreds of people were slaughtered.

When Belalcázar heard about Alvarado's plot, he set out to capture Quito first. Inca general Quisquis, backed by 50,000 indigenous warriors, blocked Belalcázar's way. The locals far outnumbered the Spanish troops. But the indigenous Ecuadorans, who had been conquered by the Inca, weren't loyal to Quisquis. Why should they fight for the people who had invaded them? Many of them fled. To increase his chance of a successful invasion of Quito, Belalcázar struck a deal with Alvarado, paying him to leave Ecuador. Alvarado returned to Guatemala a much richer man.

When Belalcázar finally reached Quito, the city lay in ruins. The Inca had burned it down and deserted it. Belalcázar claimed Quito for Spain, and a few years later he captured and claimed the coastal town of Guayaquil. Within 15 years, the Spanish had completed their conquest of Ecuador. Tens of thousands of indigenous people died in battle, from starvation, or from disease.

Sebastián de Belalcázar led the Spanish conquest of Ecuador.

A Colonial Hero

Francisco Eugenio de Santa Cruz y Espejo (1747–1795) was a doctor, lawyer, and writer. As the editor of a newspaper in Quito, he inspired the separatist movement, encouraging citizens to break away from Spain and be independent. He was jailed for his views and later forced to leave Ecuador. He also wrote extensively about health care, particularly methods of preventing the deadly disease smallpox. Espejo is considered a hero among Ecuadorans, and his image appeared on the old 500-sucre banknote and many coins.

Early Colonial Years

Spanish priests and settlers followed the conquistadores, and Spain divided its new property between settlers and the church. The Catholic Church played a huge part in developing the Spanish community. It built churches and convents, schools and libraries. Missionaries forced many indigenous people to adopt Christianity.

The government in Spain gave property to Spanish settlers in Ecuador under a system called *encomienda*. The settlers were given the land in exchange for defending it against invaders and helping convert the indigenous people to the Catholic religion. Indigenous people who refused to convert or to work for the Spanish were beaten and put in prison.

The Spanish required all indigenous people to work. Men labored in the fields and tended livestock. Women and children spent long hours in textile workshops where they

wove wool into cloth. Poor working conditions and European diseases such as smallpox killed many indigenous people. Yet many survived the brutal treatment. And eventually some organized and rose up against their oppressors.

Ecuadoran society developed several different classes. The people with the most power had been born in Spain. They were called *peninsulares*. Below them were *criollos*—people of Spanish descent born in Ecuador. Next came mestizos, who had a mixed Spanish and indigenous background. The people with the least power in Ecuadoran society were the indigenous people, the descendants of the original Ecuadorans.

Two Principal Cities

Since colonial times, Ecuador has had two principal cities, Quito and Guayaquil (left). Quito is the country's administrative capital and is located in the northern Sierra region. Guayaquil lies to the south along the coast. It is the financial, agricultural, and shipping center of Ecuador.

Independence

In the early 1800s, after about 300 years of Spanish control, indigenous people, mestizos, and some people of Spanish descent revolted against Spain. They wanted to decide for themselves how to live and how to manage their business and government. They wanted independence from Spain.

In 1809, colonists in Quito led an unsuccessful rebellion. But their desire for independence continued. In 1820, rebels kicked Spanish leaders out of the port city of Guayaquil. Violence and protest became common throughout the country. Finally, in 1822, rebel forces under the leadership of Antonio José de Sucre achieved victory, defeating the Spanish at the Battle of Pichincha. After this, Ecuador joined the newly independent Republic of Colombia, or Gran Colombia, which also included Venezuela and Panama. In 1830, the Republic of Colombia fell apart, and Ecuador declared independence.

Gran Colombia in 1830

- Gran Colombia, 1819–1830
- Ecuador, 1831
- ☉ National capital
- New Granada, 1831
- Venezuela, 1831
- ★ Department capital

Present-day Ecuador

Power Struggles

Once Ecuador became independent, conservatives and liberals battled to control it. The conservatives were centered in Quito. Many conservatives owned large tracts of land and relied on forced indigenous labor. They wanted to maintain their traditional power in society, and they also wanted to keep some ties to Spain. They believed that European-style government and society, in which the elites ruled, created stability.

The liberals, on the other hand, looked to newly independent countries like the United States of America as their model for a new society. They did not think power should be concentrated in the hands of the elites, and they wanted to limit the power of the Catholic Church, too. Many liberals were merchants and professionals. They were based in Guayaquil.

Juan José Flores was a leader in the struggle for independence. He also served three terms as president of Ecuador.

Two military men alternated power during the republic's early days. General Juan José Flores of Quito, who had fought for independence, became the Republic of Ecuador's first president in 1830. He was very concerned about maintaining control, and his government was often cruel. Vincent Rocafuerte of Guayaquil, the leader of the liberals, took over the presidency in 1835. Under Rocafuerte, Ecuador built schools and hospitals. When he left office, Flores returned to power, but in 1848, a rebellion forced him from the country.

During the next 15 years, Ecuador was in political chaos. Eleven different governments held power, and three constitutions were drafted. Civil wars broke out, and Ecuador also fought border wars with Peru and Colombia. This confusing

President Gabriel García Moreno increased the power of the Catholic Church during his time in office. He also improved education and allowed more people to vote.

and unstable time called for strong leadership. The leader who stepped up was Gabriel García Moreno, a conservative from Quito.

After Moreno became president in 1861, he demanded total power for himself and the Catholic Church. He allowed only practicing Catholics to vote. He also censored the press. During Moreno's presidency, many hospitals, schools, and roads were built. He also started work on a railroad linking Quito and Guayaquil. Moreno served as president two times before being assassinated in 1875.

After the assassination, conservatives continued to rule. A liberal was finally elected in 1897, when General Eloy Alfaro defeated the conservative candidate. He served two terms as president. During his time in power, he made many changes, including modernizing the legal code and limiting the power of the Catholic Church. He also created a public education system. Conservatives, who aligned themselves with the church, were angry that their power had diminished. A pro-church mob assassinated Alfaro in 1912.

Economic Expansion and Military Rule

The economy grew during World War I (1914–1918) as the demand increased for agricultural export products such as bananas, rice, sugar, and cocoa. The government expanded the transportation infrastructure by building new roads, bridges, and railways. By 1920, however, an economic depression had ended the expansion. Demand for agricultural products declined. People rioted in the streets to protest the rising price of goods.

In 1925, the army took control of the country in an attempt to bring order to rising chaos. But chaos would continue for some time to come. In fact, 22 presidents would come and go by 1948.

In the decades that followed, the military controlled the government twice. The first time, under General Guillermo Rodríguez Lara, lasted from 1963 to 1969. Rodríguez tried to institute social and economic reforms. Under his leadership, Ecuador began land reform, breaking up large estates that had been established under colonial rule and giving land to the people.

Workers load bananas onto a boat in Guayaquil in 1955. Bananas have long been one of the country's major export crops.

The second period of military rule occurred between 1972 and 1979. During this period, U.S. companies began pumping oil in Ecuador. Ecuador became the second-largest oil exporter in Latin America, trailing only Venezuela.

Oil profits helped the Ecuadoran economy. Meanwhile, the government borrowed a lot of money from foreign countries, using future oil profits as a guarantee that they would repay their debt. The international loans helped fund social programs and modernize transportation. But borrowing against future profits was a gamble, because oil prices do not remain stable. When the price of oil fell, the government did not have enough money to repay its debts. To do so, the government had to raise taxes and increase the cost of many goods and services.

An oil pipeline runs through the rain forest in Ecuador. The nation began exporting oil in 1972.

In 1998, President Alberto Fujimori (right) of Peru shakes hands with President Jamil Mahuad of Ecuador to commemorate the end of a 150-year border dispute between their countries.

Struggling Democracy

In 1979, a civilian government again took over. Ecuadorans elected Jaime Roldós Aguilera, who at age 38 was the youngest president in Latin America. Roldós faced many challenges. Most important, he had to reduce government spending, which made him unpopular. His own father-in-law, who was a leader in Congress, blocked many of his plans. Meanwhile, the military was threatening the presidency once again, and a dispute along the border with Peru took the attention away from economic problems.

In 1995, the border dispute with Peru became an actual war. Fighting continued for several weeks. Much of the disputed region was rich in coffee, gold, and oil. A treaty in 1998 called for joint development plans, in which both countries could profit from the territory.

El Loco

When Abdalá Bucaram (1952–) entered politics, he was considered a charming man and an excellent athlete. He had competed as a sprinter on Ecuador's 1972 Olympic team. When Bucaram ran for president in 1996, he nicknamed himself "El Loco" ("The Crazy One"). His slogan was *"Primero los Pobres,"* meaning "First the Poor." The citizens believed him and elected him president.

But the poor did not prosper under Bucaram. Instead, he raised prices for public transportation, electricity, and gas. Then he stole US$26 million from the government and took off for Panama. To many Ecuadorans, it seemed that Bucaram's nickname was accurate, and Congress soon removed him from office on the grounds of mental instability. Bucaram was formally charged with taking the money but has never been brought back to Ecuador to stand trial. The money has never been recovered.

Into the Future

In 2008, Ecuadoran voters approved a new constitution. It includes new environmental protection policies and labor laws that prohibit hiring children under the age of 15. It also requires students to finish high school and allows indigenous communities to form their own territorial administrative districts.

Since Ecuador achieved independence from Spain in 1830, more than 90 governments have come and gone. On average, each government has had about two years in power. That isn't much time to create lasting change.

Still, independent Ecuador's history has been marked by improvements in transportation and education, the rise of a middle class, and the creation of labor unions. Indigenous peoples have formed political groups to demand rights to their own land and culture. Many Ecuadorans remain hopeful that progress will continue.

In 2008, Ecuadorans voted to approve a new constitution. Here, a woman in Cayambe casts her ballot.

Democracy in Action

A CONSTITUTION DEFINES THE LAWS BY WHICH A country is run. It also provides a framework for how a government will be organized. Ecuador has had 20 constitutions. The United States, in contrast, has had just one constitution. As various presidents and military leaders assumed power in Ecuador, many of them threw out existing constitutions and rewrote them according to their beliefs about how the country should be run.

Ecuador's 2008 constitution was written under the administration of President Rafael Correa. The new constitution gave the president more power over the economy; guaranteed respect for human rights; and stated that all citizens have the same rights, regardless of age, gender, religion, race, or sexual orientation. The rights of indigenous people were expanded in the new constitution. For example, Spanish is Ecuador's official

Opposite: **Officials stand during the opening of a session of Ecuador's National Congress.**

Rafael Correa

Rafael Correa was sworn in as Ecuador's president in January 2007. He was born in Guayaquil in 1963. Before becoming president, Correa was a government economy minister and economics professor. He speaks several languages in addition to Spanish, including the indigenous language Quichua, French, and English.

language, but the constitution states that the indigenous languages Quichua and Shuar are official "intercultural languages" and that other indigenous languages can be used in indigenous schools and communities. The constitution also protects the rights of indigenous groups to practice traditional medicine and other customs. In addition, it makes protecting the environment a priority.

Ecuador is a republic, a type of government in which citizens elect their leaders. The constitution divides the national government into three branches: executive, legislative, and judicial.

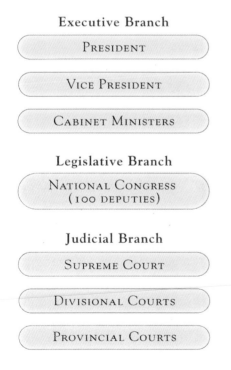

NATIONAL GOVERNMENT OF ECUADOR

Executive Branch

PRESIDENT

VICE PRESIDENT

CABINET MINISTERS

Legislative Branch

NATIONAL CONGRESS
(100 DEPUTIES)

Judicial Branch

SUPREME COURT

DIVISIONAL COURTS

PROVINCIAL COURTS

The Executive Branch

The head of the executive branch is the president, who is elected by popular vote. The president serves a four-year term. A president can serve more than one term but cannot serve two terms in a row. The president is both chief of state and head of the government. As chief of state, the president can declare war and peace. As head of the government, the president has many responsibilities, including upholding the constitution, maintaining national security and citizens' rights, and keeping the economy strong. The president must be Ecuadoran by birth and at least 35 years

President Rafael Correa (right) oversees a meeting of the national council of state security.

old at the time of the election. The president is assisted by a vice president, who is elected at the same time.

The executive branch also includes 28 cabinet ministries, each with a different area of responsibility, such as foreign affairs, tourism, and mines and petroleum. Each ministry is headed by a cabinet minister who advises the president. The president appoints the ministers, who must be Ecuadoran by birth, legal citizens, and at least 30 years old.

The executive branch controls the military, which consists of an army, a navy, an air force, and national police. All Ecuadoran men must register with the military. They are eligible to serve at age 20 and are drafted through a lottery system. Those who are drafted must serve for one year.

The National Congress is located in Quito.

The Legislative Branch

The legislative branch is the lawmaking part of government. Ecuador's legislative body, the National Congress, has 100 members, who are called deputies. Deputies pass laws, set taxes, and approve the annual budget, which is prepared by the executive branch. The Congress is also responsible for appointing members of the judicial branch. Deputies must be at least 30 years old at the time of their election and Ecuadoran by birth.

The Judicial Branch

The judicial branch consists of judges who interpret the laws in courts. Ecuador has a Supreme Court; 15 divisional courts, which hear appeals from lower courts; and 40 provincial courts. The judicial branch also includes the Fiscal Tribunal, which solves conflicts concerning taxes, and the Contentious

Administrative Tribunal, which is primarily responsible for resolving problems arising in government.

Judges must be Ecuadoran citizens by birth. They must be at least 40 years old, hold a doctoral degree in law, and have at least 15 years of professional experience as a lawyer, judge, or law professor. Justices of the Supreme Court are appointed by Congress for life.

Local Government

The Republic of Ecuador is divided into 24 provinces. The nation's president appoints a governor to run each province. Each province is further divided into 226 cantons (municipalities), which are subdivided into parishes. The president

An attorney (left) addresses a court during a trial in the Amazon town of Lago Agrio.

National Pride

The top half of Ecuador's flag is yellow. The bottom half consists of two horizontal stripes, one blue and one red. The flag design hails back to Gran Colombia, which was formed in 1821 by Ecuador, Colombia, and Venezuela. Yellow symbolizes Ecuador's former association with Gran Colombia, blue stands for independence from Spain, and red represents courage. In the center of the

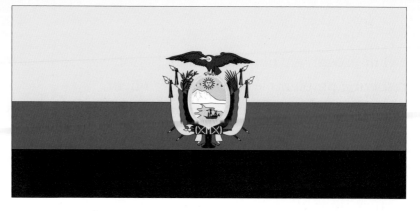

flag is a coat of arms that features Mount Chimborazo (the nation's highest peak), the first steamboat built in Ecuador, and the condor, Ecuador's national bird.

National Anthem

Juan León Mera wrote the lyrics to "¡Salve, Oh Patria!" ("We Salute You, Our Homeland!") in 1865. Antonio Neumane wrote the music the following year. The song was adopted as the national anthem in 1886.

Spanish Lyrics

Salve, Oh Patria, mil veces!
¡Oh Patria, Gloria a ti! ¡Gloria a ti!
Y a tu pecho, tu pecho, rebosa
Gozo y paz ya tu pecho rebosa;
Y tu frente, tu frente radiosa
Más que el sol contemplamos lucir,
Y tu frente, tu frente radiosa
Más que el sol contemplamos lucir.

Los primeros los hijos del suelo
que, soberbio; el Pichincha decora
te aclamaron por siempre señora
y vertieron su sangre por ti.
Dios miró y aceptó el holocausto,
y esa sangre fue germen fecundo
de otros héroes que, atónito, el mundo
vio en tu torno a millares surgir.

English Translation

O homeland, we greet you a thousand times!
Glory be to you, O homeland, glory be to you!
Your breast overflows with joy and peace,
And we see your radiant face shining
More brightly than the sun.
And we see your radiant face shining
More brightly than the sun.

The worthy sons of the soil
Which Pichincha on high is adorning,
Always acclaimed you as sovereign lady
And shed their blood for you.
God observed and accepted the sacrifice,
And that blood was the prolific seed
Of other heroes whom the world in astonishment
Saw arising in thousands around you.

President Rafael Correa meets with a group of U.S. officials to discuss trade relations. The United States is Ecuador's main trading partner.

appoints a political chief to run each canton and a political lieutenant to run each parish. The Ministry of National Defense administers the Galápagos Islands.

Each province and canton also has a council whose members are elected by popular vote. The councils maintain public services and inform the central government of budget expenditures.

Foreign Relations

Ecuador works with other countries to solve international problems and gets help from other countries to solve its own problems. For example, Ecuador and Peru long disputed control of an area of the Amazon that has valuable gold and oil deposits. The leaders of Ecuador and Peru wanted a lasting solution to the dispute, so they asked other countries to help them solve their conflict through a peaceful negotiation.

The United States, Brazil, Argentina, and Chile worked with Ecuador and Peru to draft a peace treaty, which was signed in 1998. Today, this 30-mile (48 km) border area along the Amazon is being developed to benefit both Peru and Ecuador.

Quito: Did You Know This?

Quito, the capital of Ecuador, sits at an elevation of 9,350 feet (2,850 m) in central Ecuador. Towering above the city are snowcapped mountains, and an active volcano, Pichincha, rises west of the city. The city boasts mild weather most of the year. The average temperature ranges from 59°F to 75°F (15° to 24°C) year-round.

With a population of about 1.4 million people, Quito is Ecuador's second-largest city, after Guayaquil.

Quito is also the nation's cultural center, and it is one of the best-preserved Spanish colonial cities in all of Latin America. There are so many beautiful churches, cathedrals, and convents in the old part of town that the United Nations declared it a World Cultural Heritage Site. One highlight is the Basilica (right). Another is the Church of the Society of Jesus, which was built between 1605 and 1768. Its altars are covered in gold leaf, and many fine paintings adorn the vaulted ceilings.

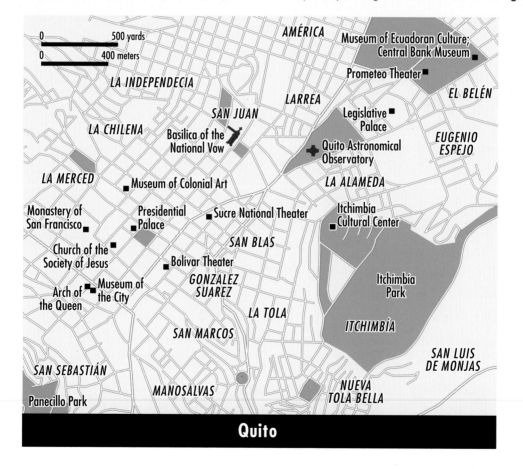

Quito

From Bananas to Oil

AGRICULTURE HAS BEEN THE MAINSTAY OF ECUADOR'S economy for most of the country's history. Coffee, bananas, and cacao, which is used to make chocolate, have long been important agricultural products. In recent decades, the country has also had a strong manufacturing sector. An industrial development law passed in 1965 helped establish factories that make such items as textiles, medicines, and appliances.

Opposite: **Ecuador is one of the world's leading producers of bananas.**

Autoworkers assemble a car at a factory in Quito.

The Oil Industry

The most important addition to Ecuador's economy in the last 40 years has been the development of the oil, or petroleum, industry. Oil was discovered in the Oriente region in 1967. In 1970, a pipeline was completed across the Andes, connecting the oil-rich Oriente to the port of Esmeraldas. After this, the country's economy grew substantially. Economic growth allowed the government to build new roads, improve education, and expand public health programs. Today, oil accounts for nearly half of Ecuador's exports and about half the government's income.

Large pipelines carry oil from drilling sites deep in Ecuadoran rain forests to the coast, where much of it is exported.

Dollars and Sucres

During the late 1990s, Ecuador experienced its worst depression in 70 years. Many banks closed, and inflation was out of control. To help stabilize the economy, Ecuador's government made the U.S. dollar its official currency in January 2000. The government had to switch to the dollar in order to receive loans from the International Monetary Fund (IMF), a major international loan agency. A rise in oil prices combined with an IMF loan and the move to the dollar did, indeed, help the economy. The dollar remains the nation's official currency.

Prior to the adoption of the dollar, Ecuador's currency was called the sucre. It was named after Antonio José de Sucre, a leader of the independence movement in the 1800s. His image appeared on the five-sucre note.

Although the Ecuadoran economy relies on oil, it is difficult to remove oil from the land without harming the environment. The oil lies deep inside the earth. Oil producers must cut down trees to make roads and to drill wells. By cutting forests, the oil companies devastate land, and oil spills pollute rivers and forests. But with care, the damage can be minimized.

The Ecuadoran government has laws protecting the land, but these laws are not always followed. Ecuadoran citizens have also tried to protect the land themselves. Indigenous people have often protested drilling in the rain forest.

Above: The coffee plant produces red fruit. Inside the fruit are seeds, or beans, that are used to make coffee.

Resources

Forests	Ag	Silver	NG	Natural gas
Livestock	Au	Gold	⚒	Oil
Tropical crops	Cd	Cadmium	Pb	Lead
Upland crops	Cem	Cement	Sn	Tin
Nonagricultural land	Cu	Copper	Zn	Zinc

Agriculture

Agriculture is the second-largest segment of the economy. Forty percent of the country's export earnings come from crops. Ecuador is the world's top supplier of bananas. Banana farms spread out around the city of Machala on the southern coast. Coffee and cacao are also important crops grown for export.

Growing flowers is a booming business in Ecuador. The cut-flowers industry requires a large number of people to tend the fields. Most workers in the industry are women. They harvest the flowers and pack them for shipping. Men generally water and fertilize the fields. Roses are the most profitable crop. Most are grown in Cotopaxi Province, where sunny days and cool mountain air provide ideal conditions. About a billion roses are raised in Ecuador every year. Many of them are sold to the United States and Europe.

A worker harvests roses on a farm in northern Ecuador. Ecuador is the third-largest flower exporter in the world.

Greener Roses

To encourage Ecuadoran growers to raise flowers without using so many pesticides, a firm in Germany provides a "Green Seal" to those with more environment- and employee-friendly practices. Limiting the use of chemical pesticides to kill insects helps protect the land and workers' health. The Green Seal attracts buyers who are seeking fair-trade products. Generally, companies selling such products pay their workers a fair wage, provide good working conditions, and care for their land.

In addition to large-scale farming operations, Ecuador has many small farms. A 1964 law broke up large farms and gave small plots of land to local people. Those plots are about 12 acres (5 ha) in size. The people who farm them typically grow enough food for their families with perhaps a bit left over to sell at local markets. Their crops include corn, potatoes, barley, and beans.

What Ecuador Grows, Makes, and Mines	
Agriculture	
Bananas (2004)	4.7 million metric tons
Cacao (2004)	111,000 metric tons
Coffee (2001)	63,720 metric tons
Manufacturing	
Lumber (2003)	600,000 cubic meters
Refined sugar (2002)	523,000 metric tons
Residual fuel oils (2005)	3,492 metric tons
Mining	
Crude petroleum (2005)	250,000 metric tons
Natural gas (2005)	46,000 metric tons
Clays (2004)	9,000 metric tons

Seafood

Many Ecuadorans raise shrimps in swampy saltwater areas. Shrimp farming started in Ecuador in the 1980s. Today, shrimps are Ecuador's number-three export product, after oil and bananas. Ecuador is one of the main shrimp suppliers to the world and the largest in Latin America.

Mangrove trees are often destroyed to start shrimp ponds along the shore. This has caused trouble for the fishing industry, because most baby fish begin their lives amid the protected area in the mangrove roots. Mangroves also protect shorelines from storm damage. It is estimated that nearly 60 percent of Ecuador's mangrove habitats have been destroyed to create shrimp farms, and it takes about 100 years for the mangroves to recover. Environmentalists are working to develop ways to build shrimp ponds without destroying mangroves.

Weights and Measures

Ecuador uses the metric system. Here are some common U.S. measures and their metric equivalents:
1 inch = 2.54 centimeters
1 pound = 0.45 kilograms
1 gallon = 4.5 liters

A worker cuts a log in the rain forest. Forestry employs about 6 percent of Ecuadoran workers.

Fishing is also an important industry in Ecuador. Tuna is the number-one fish caught for export. Huge fishing boats troll the seas for days. Once fish are caught, they are refrigerated on board the boat. This helps keep the fish fresh for both local and international customers. After the fishing boats return to port, the fish are boxed for export. The main fishing ports are on the central and southern coasts.

Forestry

Balsa wood has been important to Ecuadorans since ancient times. The region's first known sailors, the Manta, built their rafts out of balsa wood. The lightweight wood floats well and is very strong. Today, Ecuador is a major exporter of balsa wood.

Most Ecuadoran lumber is used domestically. Many coastal homes are built of bamboo. In the highlands, pine and eucalyptus trees are used for fuel and in construction. Latex, gum, and palm tree products, such as hearts of palm, an edible tender shoot of the plant, also come from trees.

Manufacturing

Most of what Ecuador makes is used in the country. Manufactured products include lumber, refined sugar, residual fuel oils, cement, chocolate, pasta, bread, meat, and instant coffee. Ecuador exports canned meats, fruit drinks, textiles, ceramics, and leather to neighboring countries.

Many textile factories are located in and around the capital city, Quito. The nearby town of Otavalo is known for its crafts market and beautiful weaving. The weavers in Otavalo export woven rugs, belts, ponchos, and tapestries.

A weaver in Otavalo creates a boldly patterned carpet.

Panama hats are a significant export product. They are woven from a thick grass called toquilla straw, which grows along the coast. It can take up to three months to make a good-quality hat. The best come from Montecristi, a town along the central coast. The finest custom-made Panama hat, called a *superfino*, can cost up to US$3,000.

Mining

Deep under the ground in Ecuador lie valuable metals such as gold, silver, copper, lead, cadmium, and zinc. Natural gas and clay are also produced in Ecuador.

Gold originally brought Spanish conquistadores to Ecuador. The precious metal has been mined in Ecuador for centuries. Much of it today comes from Nambija mining district, in the southern Sierra. Gold mining is a difficult and dangerous job. Because of heavy rains, mines in the southeastern regions sometimes collapse and trap miners inside.

Hats with a Mistaken Identity

Panama hats are traditional straw hats with brims. Despite their name, they originated in Ecuador. In the mid-1800s, many of these Ecuadoran hats were shipped to the United States from Panama. Americans mistakenly thought the hats were Panamanian and began calling them Panama hats. As they grew in popularity, the name stuck. But to this day, they are made in Ecuador.

A tourist and a guide use a canoe to explore the rain forest. Nearly a million tourists travel to Ecuador every year.

Service Industries

About half of Ecuadoran workers have service-related jobs. Tourism and transportation lead the services sector.

The Galápagos Islands get the bulk of visitors to Ecuador. More than 100,000 people visit them each year. Tourism to the mainland rose in the early 2000s, as visitors explored the mountains, the rain forests, and Ecuador's historic cities. The government has encouraged mainland tourism by improving airports and key destinations such as Guayaquil's waterfront.

The City of Manta

About 2,000 years ago, indigenous people called the seaside city of Manta Jocay, which means "House of Fish." Lots of fish live in the coastal waters, and they were a source of food for the ancient Manteños. These people were especially known for their pottery and skills navigating at sea. They were also expert raft builders. They made rafts from lightweight balsa wood, which floats easily in water.

In 1535, when Spanish conquerors arrived, the Spaniard Francisco Pacheco renamed the city Manta.

Today, it is among Ecuador's top tourist destinations. Gold, silver, and stone artifacts of the ancient Manta culture are on display in the Central Bank Museum. Tourists who visit Manta can soak up the sun on its beautiful stretch of beach by day and dine and dance at night. About 180,000 people live in the city.

Manta is the second-largest port in Ecuador, after Guayaquil. Hundreds of tuna boats ply the waters off the coast and then ship their catch from Manta to international destinations.

Foreign Exchange

Guayaquil is the nation's main port. Other major ports include Esmeraldas, Manta, Puerto Bolívar, and La Libertad. International airports are located near Quito and Guayaquil. Many rivers, including the Guayas, Daule, and Vinces, are used as transportation routes. Ecuador has about 27,000 miles (43,000 km) of roads. The nation's most developed road network is near the coast. This includes the Pan-American Highway, which runs through the country from north to south. Buses travel the highways and smaller roads, connecting towns and cities.

The Pan-American Highway cuts through the Andes Mountains, making bus and car travel in the rugged region possible.

A Tapestry
of Peoples

I F YOU LOOK AT A TAPESTRY FROM A DISTANCE, YOU SEE A complete picture. Look at it up close, and you see that many different threads create that picture. The same is true when you look at Ecuador's ethnic groups. Each group is like a thread. Considering each group allows for a better understanding of its contributions to the unique tapestry that is the Ecuadoran people.

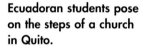

Opposite: **A girl from the mountain village of Zumbahua**

Ecuadoran students pose on the steps of a church in Quito.

Who Lives in Ecuador?

Mestizo	65%
Indigenous	25%
White	7%
Afro-Ecuadoran	3%

A Tapestry of Peoples **85**

In Ecuador, a person's class is often, but not always, tied to race. The class distinctions are a result of the Spanish colonial structure established in the 16th century. As colonizers, Spaniards were the ruling class. The indigenous people became the working class. Through time, Spanish and indigenous people had children together and a new group emerged, called mestizos. Many mestizos worked as managers on farms.

Today, people of Spanish heritage form most of the upper-income group. Many indigenous Ecuadorans live in poverty. But the majority of Ecuadorans, including most of Ecuador's small middle class, are mestizos. Most mestizo Ecuadorans live in cities. They work in all kinds of occupations. Many aspects of Ecuadoran culture have mestizo origins. For example, much Ecuadoran music combines indigenous flutes and tunes with guitars, which were brought to Ecuador by Spanish settlers.

About 25 percent of Ecuadorans are indigenous, people descended from those who were already liv-

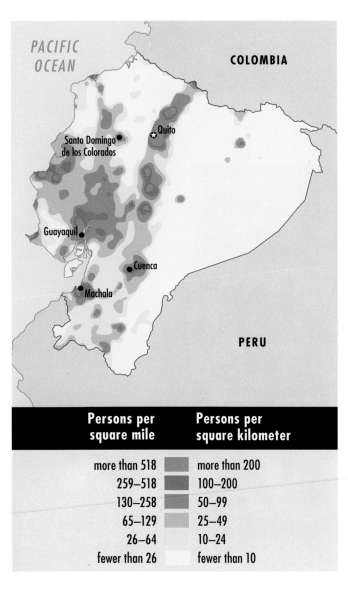

Persons per square mile		Persons per square kilometer
more than 518		more than 200
259–518		100–200
130–258		50–99
65–129		25–49
26–64		10–24
fewer than 26		fewer than 10

A woman speaks with policemen in Quito. Most people in Ecuador are mestizo.

ing in the area when the Spanish arrived. Most indigenous Ecuadorans live in the mountains. They have fought to maintain their land, languages, and cultures. They have been so successful that the 2008 constitution includes expressions in Quichua, Ecuador's most common indigenous language. It includes the statement "*Ama killa, ama llulla, ama shwa,*" an ancient Quichua behavioral code that means "Don't be lazy, don't lie, don't steal."

Population of Major Cities (2001 est.)

Guayaquil	1,985,379
Quito	1,399,378
Cuenca	599,546
Machala	204,578

Quichua mothers often carry their babies on their backs.

People of the Andes

The Quichua are the single largest indigenous group in Ecuador. They are related to the Quechua in Bolivia and Peru. Today, there are about 2 million Quichua in Ecuador. Most live in the Sierra region, but some also live in the Oriente.

Living in the Andes, the Quichua developed farming methods to match the demanding landscape. They created irrigation systems and learned to dry food in the cool mountain air. The Quichua get much of their meat, wool, and leather from llamas and alpacas—hardy mountain animals with thick fur. They also use them as pack animals, to carry items from field to home.

Quichua society depends on community members working together. Their system of mutual aid is called *ayni*. Everyone is expected to participate. If a house needs to be built, a bridge repaired, or a road cut through the forest, community members organize to get the work done. Neighbors help one another because they know that someday they, too, will need help. In some villages, people who don't work on community projects must pay a fine.

In Ecuador today, some Quichua can be recognized by their traditional clothing. Women wear a long tunic or skirt, an embroidered shirt, and a shawl. People from different

Quichua men sell ice wrapped in straw at a market in the Andes. The Quichua have a long tradition of chopping ice from the frigid Andean peaks, but the tradition is dying out.

villages wear different colors of clothing. The beads women wear also distinguish their region. Many men have stopped wearing traditional dress, except for their distinctive ponchos.

In the southern highlands is a Quichua subgroup called the Saraguro, who are closely connected to the Inca. They are easily identified because they wear mostly black. Legend has it that they wear black because they are still mourning the death of Emperor Atahualpa, who was killed by the Spanish conquistador Francisco Pizarro in 1533. The 20,000 Saraguro mainly work as cattle breeders and traders.

Southwest of Quito, about 2,000 Tsáchila live on a reserve. The Tsáchila have a distinctive look. The men make a red

About 22,000 Saraguros live in the highlands of southern Ecuador. They wear primarily black clothing.

The Otavaleño People

About 50,000 Otavaleños live in Ecuador, around Otavalo, just north of Quito. The Otavaleño people are renowned for their bold textiles, which they sell around the world. They tend to dress in their traditional clothing. Women wear long skirts with embroidered frilly white blouses. Men wear blue ponchos, white pants, and elegant Panama hats. Most Otavaleños speak Quichua as their first language. Spanish is their second language.

A Tsáchila man displays the fruit that he uses to shape and color his hair. Only Tsáchila men paint their hair.

paste out of achiote fruit and smear it onto their hair with globs of petroleum jelly. The result looks like a thin hat brim made of hair. The Tsáchila are best known for their skilled use of traditional methods to treat illnesses. People throughout Ecuador seek out Tsáchila for their healing abilities.

People of the Amazon

Some Quichua live in the Amazon. The region is also home to other distinct groups, including the Shuar, the Cofán, and the Waorani.

About 40,000 Shuar live a seminomadic life in Ecuador. They plant some crops in a base area, but they don't have permanent homes. Shuar men wear kiltlike wraps, and women wear long simple dresses. They spin thread and yarn from cotton and wool and dye it red or blue.

Working Together

The Shuar people belong to CONAIE (Confederation of Indigenous Nationalities of Ecuador), a group that represents indigenous people throughout the Amazon.

CONAIE works to protect the land rights of indigenous people. It also promotes the use of indigenous languages and tries to preserve indigenous culture.

The Shuar have the most successful political organization in the Amazon. They formed it in 1964 to represent their interests to the government and other organizations. The federation proved especially useful when oil was discovered in the Oriente.

Another group, the Cofán, live on a reserve on the northeastern border of Ecuador and Colombia. They use fire to clear land for planting crops. The Cofán make beautiful and elaborate necklaces from beads, bones, and feathers. For special occasions, they paint their faces with red dye from achiote fruit. Like the Shuar, the Cofán have organized to protect their ancestral lands. They were successful in securing approximately 1 million acres (400,000 ha) that are now protected through agreements with the government. Unlike some

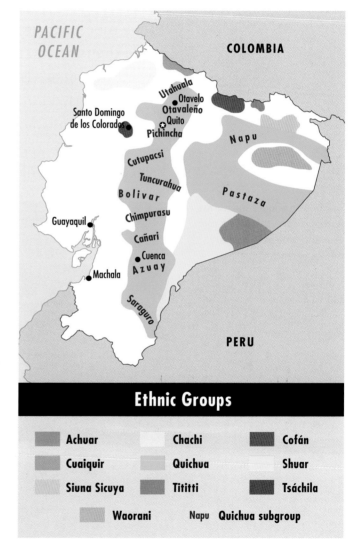

Ethnic Groups

- Achuar
- Cuaiquir
- Siuna Sicuya
- Chachi
- Quichua
- Tititti
- Waorani
- Cofán
- Shuar
- Tsáchila

Napu Quichua subgroup

other indigenous groups of the Amazon, the Cofán allow organized tour groups to visit their villages.

The Waorani, on the other hand, prefer to live undisturbed. It is estimated that about 3,000 Waorani remain in the Ecuadoran rain forest. The forest is the fabric of their life. They use blowguns to hunt their prey. A blowgun is made from a long tube, such as bamboo. A hunter places a poisoned dart inside the tube and then blows through it, propelling the dart toward its target. Traditionally nomadic, the Waorani today are more settled into forest communities. But their forest lifestyle is becoming more and more difficult as loggers and the oil industry intrude into their ancestral lands. The Waorani, too, have organized politically to save their land and culture.

The Shuar people live in the Amazon forest. Here, a man uses the leaf of a banana tree as shelter from the rain.

Many Ecuadorans of Spanish descent work in government and in businesses such as banks.

Spanish Ecuadorans

People of Spanish heritage tend to be the most educated and wealthiest group, and they hold many of the highest jobs in business and government. Many Ecuadorans of Spanish descent speak English and frequently travel to Europe and the United States.

There are regional differences among Spanish Ecuadorans. Upper-class people on the coast see themselves as different from those in the Sierra. Sierrans tend to be more conservative and reserved in nature. The people on the coast tend to be more liberal. Guayaquil is the financial center of the country, and an outgoing, energetic spirit is very much alive in that city. Quito, on the other hand, is Ecuador's cultural center. It is home to treasured museums and beautiful old churches. Religion and customs are cherished in Quito.

Afro-Ecuadorans selling vegetables at a market in Otavalo

Afro-Ecuadorans

The first people of African descent arrived in Ecuador as enslaved workers. Today, their descendants live in two main areas. The largest Afro-Ecuadoran community is along the northern coast around Esmeraldas. There is also a significant Afro-Ecuadoran community in the Andean town of Chota. Ecuadoran music shows strong African influences.

Lebanese Ecuadorans

Lebanese people first came to Ecuador in the late 19th century to work as cocoa-exporting merchants and traders. They settled mostly in Guayaquil. It is unclear how many Lebanese migrated to Ecuador at that time, but their economic and political influence has been significant. Two Lebanese Ecuadorans have been president: Jamil Mahuad and Abdalá Bucaram. In addition to political leaders, families of Lebanese descent have produced some of Ecuador's most successful businesspeople.

Jamil Mahuad is one of two Lebanese Ecuadorans who have become president. He served as president from 1998 to 2000.

Chinese Ecuadorans

In 2007, members of Ecuador's small Chinese community celebrated the opening of the first Chinese school founded by people living in Ecuador.

Chinese people first came to Ecuador in the 1800s to work building the Guayaquil-Quito railway. Through the years, their descendants have worked as miners, farmers, and fishers. Today, there is a large Chinese community in the coastal town of Quevedo.

Spanish is the dominant language in Ecuador. On January 21, 2009, Spanish-language newspapers in Quito announced the inauguration of U.S. president Barack Obama.

Languages

Spanish is the official language of Ecuador. It is the primary language used in schools, government, and daily life. The new constitution drafted in 2008 made the indigenous languages Quichua and Shuar official "intercultural" languages. This action both shows respect for indigenous groups and acknowledges the reality of life for many indigenous people, who learn their own, local language first and Spanish second.

Speaking Spanish

There are 29 letters in the Spanish alphabet. Spanish does not use the letter *k* or *w*, but *ch*, *ll*, *rr*, and *ñ* are counted as separate letters.

In Spanish, vowels are always pronounced the same way:

a is pronounced as it is in "cat"

e is pronounced as in "let"

i is pronounced like "*ee*" in "seek"

o is pronounced as in "boat"

u is pronounced as in "dude"

Many consonants are pronounced like English letters. Here are some key differences:

ll is like the *y* in "yacht"

ñ is like the *ni* in "onion"

rr is a strong "*r*" sound vibrated on the tongue

h is silent

j is like the *h* in "he"

qu is like the *k* in "kind"

Active Faith

The Roman Catholic Church has had a strong influence on Ecuadorans since the 16th century. The church held a lot of political power during colonial days. Church and state were not separate at that time. The church owned land, controlled behavior with strict religious beliefs, and worked hard to convert the indigenous peoples. In 1904, the Ecuadoran government introduced freedom of religion. Since then, Ecuadorans have been able to practice whatever faith they choose.

Opposite: **Churches are often the dominant buildings in Ecuadoran towns. The beautiful Jordan Church is in Otavalo.**

The vast majority of Ecuadorans are Catholic. Here, Ecuadorans attend mass at the Cathedral of Quito.

Religions in Ecuador

Roman Catholicism	95%
Protestantism	4%
Judaism	less than 1%
Islam	less than 1%
Buddhism	less than 1%

Accepting the Catholic Faith

Catholicism remains strong in Ecuador. Most people carry a picture of the Virgin Mary, the mother of Jesus Christ, in their wallets. And most Ecuadorans take part in ceremonies that confirm their commitment to their faith. The first of these is baptism. During a baptism, godparents hold the baby

The Oldest Church

The capital city, Quito, has 86 churches. The most spectacular is the Church of the Society of Jesus, the largest colonial building in Quito and the oldest church in South America. Construction began on the church in 1605 and took 163 years to complete. It is a masterpiece of Spanish colonial architecture. The exterior columns were hand carved. Inside, the altars are covered in gold leaf, and the walls and ceiling are adorned with murals. A painting of the Virgin Mary is the most valuable piece of art in the church. It is decorated with glimmering emeralds and glistening gold leaf. The painting is kept in a vault and brought out only on special occasions.

The Lady of Quito

The tomb of Mariana Paredes y Flores sits at the foot of the altar inside the spectacular Church of the Society of Jesus in Quito. Hers is a tragic story. In 1645, Quito was plagued with disasters. Earthquakes and quickly spreading diseases claimed the lives of many people.

At the height of the tragedies, Mariana was 26 years old. She prayed, asking that her life be taken to spare the lives of others. She soon became very ill. At the time, bloodletting, or draining some blood from a sick person, was a common medical practice. Some of Mariana's blood was let and then poured in the garden outside her home. When she died a few months later, lilies bloomed where her blood had been spilled. At the same time, the city's problems were fading. Some people considered these two events miracles. Mariana was made a saint and became known as the Lady of Quito. Her story remains a strong part of Quito's religious culture.

while a priest blesses the baby with holy water. The ritual is a symbol of the child's becoming a full member of the church. Godparents are like second parents. They participate in religious and other celebrations and help guide a child in life.

Festivals and Saints

Many holidays in Ecuador have elements of both Catholicism and indigenous religion. For example, the Feast of Saint John the Baptist, which peaks on June 24, is a major event in the Otavalo region. People dress up in costumes and parade and dance every night for a week. This holiday likely replaced the Inca holiday Inti Raymani, which was celebrated on June 21.

Another blended holiday, All Souls' Day, known as the Day of the Dead in Ecuador, takes place on November 2. In Ecuador, the indigenous tradition includes honoring the dead with offerings of food. Traditional indigenous religions say that the souls of the dead return to the earth for 24 hours and

An Ecuadoran woman visits a cemetery on the Day of the Dead.

need food and water. On the Day of the Dead, special breads are placed on the graves of departed loved ones. People also make small altars inside their homes. They place favorite items on these altars in remembrance.

Expanding Faith

In addition to the Roman Catholic Church, other Christian groups have also made their way into Ecuador. Among them is a ministry that broadcasts Christian programming on its own radio station. Based in Quito, radio station HCJB aired its first program on Christmas Day in 1931. The call letters stand for Heralding Christ Jesus' Blessings. It was the first Christian radio station in the world. Since then, HCJB has established missionary radio stations worldwide. Its programming is also heard on the Internet. HCJB is interdenominational, meaning that it has members from many Christian groups. HCJB has established hospitals, mobile medical units, and clinics in several places in Ecuador.

Several Protestant groups are active in Ecuador, including Pentecostals, Jehovah's Witnesses, Mormons, and Baptists. Some Ecuadorans also practice Buddhism, Judaism, and Islam.

Major Religious Holidays

Easter	March or April
Saint John the Baptist	June 24
Saints Peter and Paul	June 29
Festival of the Virgin of Mercy	September 23–24
Day of the Dead	November 2
Christmas Eve	December 24
Christmas Day	December 25

A group of evangelical Protestants sing and play music outside a church in Quito.

Indigenous Religious Beliefs

In ancient indigenous customs, Pachamama, or Mother Earth, gives life. Taita Inti is Father Sun. Mother Earth revolves around Father Sun. She is nourished by the sun and gives life to plants, animals, and people.

For the indigenous peoples of the Sierra, the mountains are thought to have strong spiritual powers. The mountains are said to give power to shamans, people believed to be able to cure illness and communicate with spirits. Shamans are sometimes referred to as the husband or wife of a mountain.

In indigenous religions, shamans help communicate with the spirits. Here, shamans perform a ritual in front of the Monastery of San Francisco in Quito.

Dancing for Mother Earth

In the festivals that take place around the winter and summer solstices, the shortest and longest days of the year, dancing is part of the ritual. In these dances, people stomp their feet and move in circular patterns. The movements are said to prepare the earth for a new season of crops. They are also an invitation to Mother Earth to join the dance. In the picture to the left, shamans prepare for a solstice ritual.

Some indigenous Ecuadorans believe that people get sick because the spirits of the mountains have robbed them of their energies. When this happens, a shaman is called in to convince the spirits to leave the sick person, allowing him or her to heal.

In the rain forests of the Oriente, spirituality is tied to the forest. Animals and plants have the power to heal people and to make them sick. As in the Sierra, medicine men and women are called upon to communicate with the spirit world. Shamans hold rituals for births, deaths, and rites of passage into adulthood. They use drums, feathers, and rocks in their ritual ceremonies.

CHAPTER NINE

Sights, Sounds, Sports

It is said that at an Ecuadoran fiesta, or party, everyone dances. That includes grandmothers, grandfathers, babies just learning to walk, parents, and teenagers. Everyone likes to move their feet. No Ecuadoran celebration is complete without music, which brings joy and a sense of connection among family and friends.

Drums and flutes are central to Ecuadoran music.

The Sounds of Music

Wherever you go in Ecuador, you will likely see groups of musicians playing on street corners. Many kinds of instruments are used in Ecuador, depending on the style of music. Traditional Andean folk musicians play wind instruments such as bamboo flutes, panpipes, and conch shells. Drums called bombos keep the rhythm along with maracas, which are rattles made from gourds. The wind instruments and melody of Andean music create a distinctly sad sound. When the Spanish arrived in Ecuador long ago, they brought with them stringed instruments such as guitars, mandolins, and violins. Andean musicians added these instruments to their groups.

Folk dancers perform at a music festival in 2007.

People descended from Africans settled around the coastal areas in Ecuador, and African musical and dance traditions continue to thrive in the region. The marimba, an instrument from Africa, is like a xylophone made from wood pieces. It is played by striking the wooden bars with mallets. The marimba is used in many types of Ecuadoran music. *Bomba negra* is a musical style that blends African rhythms and Andean melodies.

Music from the Caribbean has also influenced Ecuadoran music. Many Ecuadorans enjoy salsa, *cumbia*, and merengue, popular types of Latin dance music. Nightclubs around the country burst with Latin dance sounds. Horns blare and drums

Andean Chill

Andean chill is a style of music that combines traditional instruments of the Andes such as panpipes with modern electronic pop music styles. The hypnotic beat of Andean chill creates a trance-dance atmosphere. Miki González is considered to be one of the best Andean chill performers.

Ecuador's National Instrument

Much Ecuadoran music features a *ronda-dor*, or panpipe, an instrument unique to the Andes. The rondador consists of several bamboo or cane pipes of varying lengths, which are bound together. The musician plays the instrument by blowing into the holes of the different pipes, much as a person would play a harmonica.

add a steady beat. Rap, reggae, and Andean chill are big hits in local clubs, where young people dance the night away.

Ecuadorans who enjoy Western classical music can attend regular performances by the National Symphony Orchestra in Quito at the Sucre National Theater. Ecuadoran musicians study classical music and jazz at the National Conservatory of Music in Quito.

Masters of Cloth

The tradition of weaving cloth is thousands of years old. Today, Ecuadorans weave wool, cotton, silk, and synthetic fibers into everything from belts to blankets. Some weavers still use traditional looms and natural dyes to color their cotton and wool. Traditional designs typically feature bright blues and reds woven into geometric patterns.

Ecuadoran weavings often feature bright colors and intricate patterns.

Belts made in the Salasca region are typically made from llama wool. The signature vibrant red color comes from cochineal, a natural dye made from a crushed female bug that feeds on the red fruit of the prickly pear cactus.

Ikat is a method of dying threads similar to tie-dyeing. This process is used in cultures worldwide. In Ecuador, ikat textiles come primarily from the Cuenca region in the southern Ecuadoran Andes. People from Cuenca make shawls dyed a deep blue color with fancy fringes. The dyeing and weaving process takes only about a day, but it can take months to create the fringes.

Tapestries are pictures woven from threads. In Ecuadoran tapestries, traditional symbols, such as the Inca calendar, or rural scenes are common designs. Some tapestries are considered fine art and are hung on walls. Others are used to make wearable art clothing and accessories, including ponchos and handbags.

During Inca times, textiles were as valuable as gold and silver and were used for trade. The Spanish colonizers also appreciated the fine fabrics. In the early colonial period, Ecuadoran fabrics were far superior to European versions. Today, people from around the world travel to Ecuador to collect tapestries. Many Ecuadorans rely on weaving for their income. Men do most of the weaving, but some Ecuadoran women are also weavers.

Some Ecuadoran artisans make clothing. Many women knit gorgeous wool sweaters, vests, and hats by hand. Women at the Zuleta Embroidery Workshop, near Quito, embroider skirts, blouses, napkins, and tablecloths using colorful threads. Doña Rosario, the wife of Ecuadoran president Galo Plaza Lasso, founded the workshop in the 1940s. Embroidery has been a valuable source of income to many Zuleteño families.

Other Crafts

Many regions in Ecuador are associated with particular crafts. In Cotacachi, which is in the north, artisans make leather into everything from wallets to clothes and backpacks. People in Chordaleg, in the east, make beautiful jewelry from gold and silver. The Canelos, a subgroup of the Quichua in the Oriente, make fine ceramics. Canelo women masterfully create fine, thin ceramic bowls and pots with painted designs.

A wide variety of hand-made jewelry is available at Ecuadoran markets.

The Canelos are also accomplished wood-carvers, as are people who live in the northern town of San Antonio de Ibarra. They carve balsa wood into statues, often of birds or religious figures. They also use the wood to make handmade boxes.

Masapán, figures made of bread that are used during the Day of the Dead celebration, most often come from Calderón. The artisans dye the dough with bright colors and typically shape it into animal and human figures.

Beginning in the 1500s, when Spaniards first arrived in Ecuador, most paintings were created for churches. Artists learned to paint representations of saints and other religious subjects.

In the 20th century, a change occurred in the artistic spirit of the country's painters. The movement became known as *indigenismo*, or "indigenization" in English. The movement was defined not by a style but, rather, by a subject matter. The indigenismo artists made paintings that concerned the struggles of indigenous people. Their paintings reflected sorrow and pain. Prominent indigenismo artists include Oswaldo Guayasamín, Eduardo Kingman, and Camilo Egas.

A Popular Artist: Oswaldo Guayasamín

Oswaldo Guayasamín was born in Quito in 1919, the oldest of 10 children of a Quichua father and a mestizo mother. He loved art as a child, and he eventually attended the School of Fine Arts in Quito. He developed an expressionist style. In this style, an artist exaggerates the most important aspects of a subject. This painting is part of a series called "On Tenderness." Guayasamín, who died in 1999, remains one of the most popular artists in Ecuador.

The Central Bank Museum

The Central Bank Museum in Quito is filled with evidence of the human and natural history of Ecuador. The art and artifacts are arranged in chronological order, providing visitors the opportunity to see how arts influenced one another over time. A highlight is the Golden Court, which showcases the stunning gold work of indigenous peoples who lived hundreds of years ago. Paintings by modern indigenismo artists such as Camilo Egas and Eduardo Kingman also hang on this museum's walls.

Literature and the Press

Ecuador has a long tradition of writers who deal with social and political issues in their work. They have tried to change society with words instead of military might. In the 19th century, Juan Montalvo (1832–1889) wrote passionately against the Catholic Church and Ecuadoran leader Gabriel García Moreno. Because his writings were very critical of the government, he was forced to leave Ecuador for Colombia. When García Moreno died, Montalvo wrote, "My pen has killed him."

Jorge Icaza (1906–1978) wrote a novel called *Huasipungo* (*The Villagers*) that shocked many people with its detailed descriptions of brutality against the indigenous people. The book remains widely read. Journalist Alejandro Carrión Aguirre (1915–1992) also wrote poetry, essays, and novels and founded two magazines, one politically oriented and the other a literary publication. He received the Ecuadoran National Prize in recognition of his cultural contribution to Ecuador. Jenny Estrada (1940–) was among the first women to write for the mainstream press.

Ecuador's Joao Rojas (right) battles for the ball during a 2009 game between Ecuador and Argentina.

Sports

Soccer is the national sport in Ecuador. All over the country, young people and adults play the game whenever they get the chance. They also cheer on the local, regional, and national soccer teams. Ecuador's national soccer team qualified for the

Rafting Championships

Many fast-flowing rivers that rush down from the Andes Mountains are perfect for rafting. The International Rafting Federation held its 2005 championships on the Quijos River in eastern Ecuador. Teams from as far away as Japan and the Czech Republic flew in to participate in the competition. Women from the Czech Republic and men from Germany took the top prizes in their divisions.

World Cup, the world's most prestigious soccer tournament, in 2002 and in 2006.

Volleyball, basketball, and tennis are other popular sports. At the age of 17, tennis player Andrés Gómez (1960–) won a South American championship. During his professional career, Gómez won 21 singles and 33 doubles titles. He is now retired from the game.

A unique game played in Ecuador is *pelota de guante*, paddle ball. Players wear gloves with long, spiked paddles attached. They use the paddles to hit a heavy rubber ball. The game, which is similar to racquetball, is most commonly played in Ibarra and Quito.

Ecuador boasts tennis and golf clubs, yoga studios and health spas. Some Ecuadorans also enjoy horseback riding, swimming, and hiking.

An Olympic Champion

Jefferson Pérez (center) is often considered Ecuador's greatest athlete, but he is not a soccer player. He is a race walker. He was born in 1974. In 1996, Pérez won Ecuador's first Olympic medal when he took home the gold in the 20-kilometer event. In 2008, he won a silver medal.

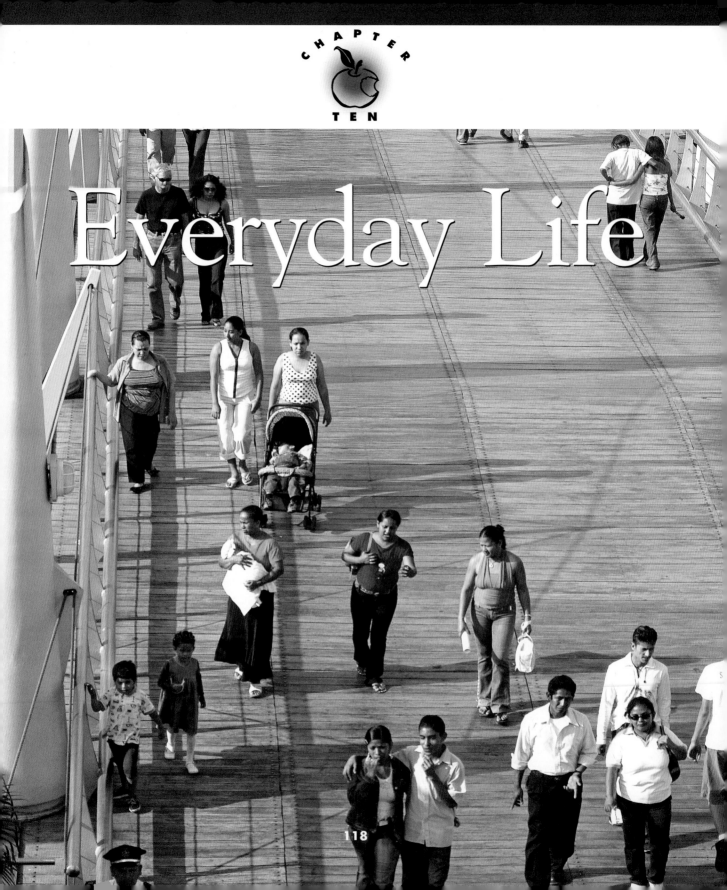

CHAPTER

TEN

Everyday Life

118

H OW PEOPLE LIVE IN ECUADOR HAS A GREAT DEAL TO do with where they live. More than half the people live in cities. Some of them live very much like people in wealthier countries, shopping in supermarkets, living in nice apartments, and hiring a maid service.

Upper- and middle-class young people in the cities have a lifestyle similar to teens in the United States or Canada. They listen to music on their MP3 players, watch satellite TV, and surf the Internet. They hang out at shopping malls and wear the latest styles. They learn English, chat on cell phones, and eat in fast food restaurants.

Country people, called *campesinos*, work hard tending fields and earn little money for their efforts. In the rain forest, many people live in small villages. They often live in a traditional way, growing or hunting the food they eat.

Opposite: **People enjoy a walk along a promenade in Guayaquil.**

Education

Ecuadoran children can start preschool as young as 4 years of age. Primary school begins at age 6 and lasts for six years. It is followed by secondary school, which lasts another six years. In secondary school, students may choose an education track that leads to college or learn a trade. The 2008 constitution requires all students to finish high school. Previously, school was mandatory only to age 14.

Many classrooms in Ecuador look much like those in the United States.

About 40 percent of children attend private school. Private schools are generally considered better than public schools because public schools often lack money to pay for teachers and equipment.

Today, about 91 percent of Ecuadorans can read and write. Most children speak at least two languages.

Ecuador has about 50 institutions of higher education. The Central University of Ecuador is the oldest university in the country. It began in 1769 as the result of a merger between the Jesuit University of Quito, established in 1651, and the Dominican University of Saint Thomas Aquinas, established in 1688. Today, the Central University offers many different fields of study, including the arts, medicine, and law. About 10,000 students attend the school.

Spinning Tops

Trompos, or tops, is a popular game. To play tops, someone draws a circle on the ground. Each player then starts a wooden top spinning in the circle. The tops bump into one another, and the stronger tops knock over the weaker ones. The winner is the owner of the last top to remain upright.

Family Life

Family is vital to Ecuadorans. In Ecuador, most people live with their families until they get married. This is especially true for women. Traditionally, the man's parents will ask the woman's parents to allow the couple to marry. This custom is called *pedir la mano* ("to ask for her hand"). In Ecuador, a civil ceremony is required for a marriage to be legal, so most people have two marriage ceremonies. The first is in a courthouse, where the chief of civil registry performs the service. The second, more elaborate ceremony is held in a church. Ecuadorans tend to marry in their late teens or early twenties, and many couples have children soon afterward.

Coming of Age

The *quinceañera* is a rite of passage that is celebrated when a girl turns 15. This celebration, which is also held in other Latin American countries, includes a church ceremony in which the girl wears a fancy dress bought especially for the occasion. After the service, everyone enjoys a huge party, complete with a special cake and gifts for the girl. Families spend as much money on a quinceañera as they would on a wedding.

Ecuadoran Names

People in many Spanish-speaking lands, including Ecuador, often have two family names, or surnames. One surname comes from the father's family name, the other from the mother's. Traditionally, the father's family name comes first. For example, in the name Juan García Estrada, García is the father's family name, and Estrada is the mother's family name. In Ecuador, parents can choose which order to put their children's surnames. Most choose the traditional order. Although most people have two surnames, many use only one. For example, Rafael Correa Delgado, the president of Ecuador, is generally called simply Rafael Correa.

A mother and her children on a rural road. The average Ecuadoran woman has 2.6 children.

Men and women tend to follow traditional gender roles. Men work, and women take care of the home and children. But this is slowly changing. More and more women are entering the workforce, and many are going to college.

Locro is a rich soup made from potatoes, cheese, and avocado.

Mealtime

In most Ecuadoran homes, breakfast is typically a light meal. A small roll with butter and jam and *café con leche* ("coffee with milk") is common.

Lunch is the largest meal of the day. Most lunches begin with soup. *Locro*, a thick soup made with fresh cheese, avocado, and potatoes, is common. *Fanesca* is a very rich soup served during Lent, the solemn period that precedes Easter. Traditionally, Catholics do not eat meat during Lent, though they do eat fish. Fanesca does not include meat, but it is rich with fish, eggs, cheese, corn, and grains. Lunch often includes rice, potatoes, and a meat or fish dish. Foods served at dinner are similar to those served at lunch, but the portions are smaller.

Ecuador is one of the world's largest producers of bananas, so it is no surprise that bananas are used in many dishes. Ecuadorans eat many different kinds of bananas, including small yellow ones, which are very sweet, and thick, small red ones that are a bit starchier. Plantains, a firm, starchy type of banana, are also common. Plantains must be cooked before eating. They are either fried or boiled and are often served as a side dish with rice and beans. Plantains are also sliced and deep fried. The result is similar to potato chips: crispy and salty.

Fried Plantains

The key to this recipe is to use a very ripe plantain. When you buy the plantain, it will probably still be somewhat green and firm to the touch. Leave it on the kitchen counter for several days until the skin starts to blacken and the fruit is soft to the touch. Have an adult nearby when you make this recipe.

Ingredients:

1 plantain
¼ cup vegetable oil
Salt to taste

Directions: Slice the plantain diagonally into thin pieces about ¼ inch (½ cm) thick. Place a small amount of oil in a frying pan and bring it to a medium heat. Fry each side of the plantain slices until browned (about 5 minutes for each side). Place on paper toweling to absorb excess oil. Sprinkle with salt. Enjoy!

Remembering the Dead

Ecuadoran law requires that a person be buried within 24 hours of death. Someone stays with the body for the entire 24 hours. After the burial, the family is in mourning. During the mourning period, they hold formal remembrance days for the dead, including November 2, the Day of the Dead. Children who are in mourning wear white clothing, and adults generally wear black and white.

Giant Christmas decorations light up Panecillo Hill in Quito.

Ecuador's National Holidays

New Year's Day	January 1
Carnival	February or March
Easter	March or April
Labor Day	May 1
Battle of Pichincha	May 24
Birth of Simón Bolívar	July 24
Independence Day	August 10
Independence of Guayaquil	October 9
Day of the Dead	November 2
Independence of Cuenca	November 3
Independence of Quito	December 6
Christmas Day	December 25

Special Occasions

The Ecuadoran celebration of Christmas includes an event called *Pase del Niño* ("Passage of the Child"). On Christmas Eve, families take a small statue of the baby Jesus to church to be blessed. In some villages, people hold a parade that includes decorated donkeys, a crib with a statue of the baby Jesus, music, and dancing. Cuenca has the largest Christmas parade in Ecuador. Children often wear costumes of biblical figures. They are accompanied by musicians and trucks decked out with shiny garlands and other ornaments.

To celebrate the New Year, many Ecuadorans dress in costumes the night before, much like the Halloween tradition in the United States. Musicians play and everyone dances. The highlight of the night is the burning of a scarecrowlike doll stuffed with sawdust and firecrackers. The doll symbolizes the old year and is burned to get rid of the bad things that happened in it and start the new year afresh. The doll is ignited at midnight. Smoke and fireworks fill the air as people dance, talk, and laugh together, looking forward to the new year.

Large papier-mâché figures stand on a street in Cuenca waiting to be bought for the New Year's celebration. During the celebration, Ecuadorans burn figures that represent evil or the past.

Timeline

Ecuador History

Ecuador becomes part of Gran Colombia.	1822
Ecuador becomes an independent republic.	1830
Gabriel García Moreno becomes president and increases the power of the Catholic Church.	1861
Ecuador establishes freedom of religion.	1904
The government begins land reform, breaking up large estates and giving land to the people.	1964
Oil is discovered in the Oriente.	1967
Ecuador and Peru fight a war over a disputed border.	1995
Ecuador suffers a severe economic crisis.	Late 1990s
Ecuador adopts the U.S. dollar as its official currency.	2000
Ecuador adopts a new constitution that includes social reforms and environmental protection policies.	2008

World History

1804	Haiti becomes independent following the only successful slave uprising in history.
1823	The United States announces the Monroe Doctrine.
1861–1865	American Civil War
1914–1918	World War I
1917	The Bolshevik Revolution brings communism to Russia.
1929	A worldwide economic depression sets in.
1939–1945	World War II
1950s–1960s	African colonies win independence from European nations.
1957–1975	Vietnam War
1989	The cold war ends as communism crumbles in Eastern Europe.
1994	South Africa abolishes apartheid.
2001	Terrorists attack the World Trade Center in New York City and the Pentagon in Arlington, Virginia.
2004	A tsunami in the Indian Ocean destroys coastlines in Africa, India, and Southeast Asia.
2008	The United States elects its first African American president.

Fast Facts

Official name: Republic of Ecuador

Capital: Quito

Official language: Spanish

Guayaquil

Ecuador's flag

Banana farm

Year of founding: 1830

National anthem: "¡Salve, Oh Patria!"
("We Salute You, Our Homeland!")

Government: Multiparty republic

Chief of state: President

Head of government: President

Area: 106,889 square miles (276,840 sq km)

**Latitude and longitude
of geographic center:** 2° S, 77°30' W

Bordering countries: Colombia to the north, Peru to the east and south

Highest elevation: Mount Chimborazo, 20,565 feet (6,268 m)

Lowest elevation: Sea level, along the Pacific coast

**Average high
temperatures:** In Quito, 66°F (19°C) in January and
67°F (19°C) in July; in Guayaquil,
88°F (31°C) in January and 84°F (29°C) in July

**Average annual
precipitation:** In Quito, 48 inches (122 cm);
in Guayaquil, 43 inches (109 cm)

**National population
(2008 est.):** 13,927,650

Church of the Society
of Jesus

Currency

**Population of largest
cities (2001 est.):**

Guayaquil	1,985,379
Quito	1,399,378
Cuenca	599,546
Machala	204,578

Famous landmarks:
- ▶ *Central Bank Museum,* Manta
- ▶ *Church of the Society of Jesus,* Quito
- ▶ *Galápagos Islands*
- ▶ *Otavalo market*
- ▶ *Sucre National Theater,* Quito
- ▶ *Yasuní National Park,* Napo

Industry: Oil is the most valuable sector of Ecuador's economy. Agriculture ranks second. Forty percent of the country's export earnings come from agricultural crops, including bananas, coffee, cacao, and flowers. Ecuador also produces fish and shrimp that are shipped around the world. Important manufactured products include lumber, processed foods, residual fuel oils, textiles, pottery, and leather.

Currency: The U.S. dollar became the official currency in 2000, replacing the sucre.

**System of weights
and measures:** Metric system

Literacy rate: 91%

Schoolchildren

Jefferson Pérez

Common Spanish words and phrases:

adiós	good-bye
hola	hello
buenos días	good morning
sí	yes
no	no
por favor	please
gracias	thank you

Famous Ecuadorans:

Alejandro Carrión Aguirre *Journalist and poet*	(1915–1992)
Rafael Correa *President*	(1963–)
Jenny Estrada *Journalist*	(1940–)
Andrés Gómez *Tennis player*	(1960–)
Oswaldo Guayasamín *Painter*	(1919–1999)
Mariana Paredes y Flores *Saint*	(1614–1645)
Jefferson Pérez *Olympic athlete*	(1974–)

To Find Out More

Books

▶ Beirne, Barbara. *The Children of the Ecuadorean Highlands*. Minneapolis, Minn.: Carolrhoda Books, 1996.

▶ Bingham, Hiram. *The Ancient Incas: Chronicles from National Geographic*. Philadelphia: Chelsea House, 1999.

▶ Blankenship, Judy. *Cañar: A Year in the Highlands of Ecuador*. Austin: University of Texas Press, 2005.

▶ Castner, James L. *Layers of Life*. New York: Benchmark Books, 2002.

▶ Gladstone, James. *Rainforest*. Secaucus, N.J.: Chartwell Books, 2006.

Web Sites

▶ **Background Note: Ecuador**
www.state.gov/r/pa/ei/bgn/35761.htm
Information about Ecuador's people, history, political conditions, and more from the U.S. State Department.

▶ **The Ecuador Channel**
www.ecuador.com
For information about attractions and events in Ecuador.

▶ **Ecuadoran-American Chamber of Commerce**
www.ecamcham.com/ecuador/
default_en.htm
An overview of Ecuador's history, geography, economic situation, transportation, and more from the country's chamber of commerce.

▶ **Guayasamín**
www.guayasamin.com/pages_ing/
index.html
Information about one of Ecuador's greatest painters, Oswaldo Guayasamín, along with a gallery of his works.

Embassies

▶ **Embassy of Ecuador**
2535 15th Street, N.W.
Washington, DC 20009
202-234-7200
www.ecuador.com

▶ **Embassy of Ecuador in Canada**
50 O'Connor St., Suite 113
Ottawa, ON K1P 6L2
Canada
613-563-8206
www.ncf.ca/ecuador

Index

Page numbers in *italics* indicate illustrations.

roadways, 46, 52, 55, 72, 73, 83, 83, 89
Rocafuerte, Vincent, 53
Rodríguez Lara, Guillermo, 55
Rojas, Joao, *116*
Roman Catholicism, 50, 53, 54, 101, *101*, 102–103, 115, 124
rondador (national instrument), 111, *111*
Rosario, Doña, 113

S

Salasca region, 112
"¡Salve, Oh Patria!" (national anthem), 66
San Antonio de Ibarra, 113
Sangay volcano, 20
San Rafael Falls, *12*, 17
Santa Cruz y Espejo, Francisco Eugenio de, 50
Santa Elena Peninsula, 43
Saraguro people, 90, *90*
service industries, 81, *81*, 83
shrimp farming, 38, 77, *77*
Shuar language, 62, 99
Shuar people, 92, 93, *94*
Sierra region, 15, 19–21, 27, 51, 80, 88, 95, 106
soccer (national sport), 116–117, *116*
Spanish conquistadores, 48, *49*, 80, 82, 90
Spanish Ecuadorans, 51, 52, 86, 95, *95*
Spanish language, 61–62, 91, 99, *99*
Spanish settlers, 50, 86, 109, 112
sports, 116–117, *116*, *117*
Sucre, Antonio José de, 52, 73

sucre (currency), 50, *50*, 73, *73*
Sucre National Theater, 111
Sun God, 44, *44*
Supreme Court, 64, 65

T

tapestries, 79, 112
Temple of the Sun, 47, *47*
textile industry, 50–51, 71, 79, *79*, 91, 112, *112*
timber industry. *See* forestry.
Tomebamba, 47
tourism, 23, 38, 41, 63, 81, *81*, 82, *82*, 83, 94
towns. *See also* cities; villages.
  Baños, 22, *22*
  Cajabamba, 18
  Chordaleg, 113
  Chota, 96
  Lago Agrio, 65
  Montecristi, 80
  Otavalo, 79, *79*, 96, *100*
  Quevedo, 98
  San Antonio de Ibarra, 113
  Tulcán, 18
transportation, 23, *23*, 54, 55, 56, 58, 59, 81, 83, *83*, 98
trompos (game), 120
Tsáchila people, 90, 92, *92*
Tulcán, 18
Tungurahua volcano, *20*, 22
Tupac Yupanqui (Inca emperor), 45, 47, 48

U

United Nations, 68

V

Valdivia people, 43–44
villages. *See also* cities; towns.
  ayni system, 89
  clothing, 89–90
  Cotacachi, 113
  mangrove forests and, 38
  Pase del Niño ceremony, 126
  tourism, 94
  Zumbahua, *84*
Vinces River, 83

W

Waorani people, 23, 94
weavings, 9, 79, *79*, 91, 111–113, *112*
weights and measures, 77
wildlife. *See* amphibian life; animal life; insect life; marine life; plant life; reptilian life.
Wolf Volcano, 24
women, 9, 50–51, 75, 89, 90, 91, 92, 107, 112, 113, 115, 121, *121*, 122, *122*
World Cup soccer tournament, 117
World War I, 55

Y

Yasuní National Park, 34

Z

Zuleta Embroidery Workshop, 113
Zuleteño people, 113
Zumbahua, *84*

Meet the Author

JoAnn Milivojevic is a freelance writer and video producer who loves to travel and explore the world. She lives in Chicago, Illinois, where she meets people from many cultures. She met many Ecuadorans while researching this book and made new friends in the process. They shared their culture with her and endured her many questions.

Some even introduced her to traditional Ecuadoran food: "I've added Ecuadoran recipes to my files and look forward to treating my family and friends to some delicious Ecuadoran meals. This sharing of food, music, and cultures makes my work as a writer exciting and rewarding."

Milivojevic's writing career has allowed her to pursue her interest in world cultures. She has written other books in the Enchantment of the World series, including *Serbia*, *Bosnia*, *Czech Republic*, and *Iran*. She traveled extensively in the Caribbean while working on writing assignments for magazines and guidebooks. And although she loves the sea, sun, and sand, meeting people makes her travels worthwhile.

Milivojevic graduated from Indiana University. Before becoming a writer, she worked as a radio and TV producer. Her dog, Tolstoy, is her writing partner. He reminds her every day that roaming the great outdoors is as important to writing as tapping at the keyboard.

Photo Credits